INTIMACY

with

God

THROUGH JOURNALING

Janet Gilham

HIS WAY

Copyright © 2014 Janet Gilham

All Rights Reserved. No part of this publication may be reproduced, stored in a retrieval system, or transmitted in any form or by any means, electronic, mechanical, photocopying, recording or otherwise without the prior written permission of the publisher.

Published by: His Way Publishing

ISBN: **978-0692229088**

Unless otherwise identified Scripture quotations are taken from the NEW AMERICAN STANDARD BIBLE®, Copyright © 1960,1962,1963,1968,1971,1972,1973,1975,1977, 1995
by The Lockman Foundation. Used by permission.

Scripture quotations marked NJKV are taken from the New King James Version®. Copyright © 1982 by Thomas Nelson, Inc. Used by permission. All rights reserved.

Please note: All pronouns referring to Father, Son and Holy Spirit are capitalized, and the name of satan is not capitalized.

DEDICATION

I dedicate this book to my husband and best friend, Jimmy. He has been my greatest encourager, through the years, with my journaling. He has also been very supportive in the process of putting my journaling into this book.

Endorsements

I am so thankful that the Father has asked Janet to share with you what she has learned about *Intimacy with God through Journaling*. I am even more overjoyed that she said, "Yes!"

This book is a personal journey—very personal—a roadmap of sorts that can lead anyone (yes, even you!) into a place where you will hear your Father's voice daily. The Word of God says, "My *sheep hear My voice…" (John10:27)*. We are His sheep—His children, and He wants to communicate with us. Many times in the book of Revelation we are reminded to have ears to hear. How many times have you poured out your heart to God and thought, "Oh, if only He would answer me"? Well, He can and He will. The book you hold in your hand will give you the keys and the courage to enter into a living relationship with your Papa God. Get to know Him—really know Him. Everything in your life will be changed.

Journaling is EASY. It's a journey even children can master. In fact, the more childlike we become, the easier it is to allow the spontaneous flow of communication to come. Ask Him anything, ANYTHING! He loves when we acknowledge Him and inquire about His ways. He knows our individual personalities and how to reach our hearts with pinpoint accuracy.

As Founder of South Georgia House of Hope, I have found journaling to be one of the most important keys in freedom from addiction. As the women in our program learn to hear His voice and experience His love, the chains of addiction are broken. Trauma and abuse are healed, and true identities and destinies are revealed. Journaling is for anyone and everyone who longs to become all God has created them to be.

Jump in; you will never be the same!

Sharon Wagner
Executive Director
South Georgia House of Hope

Until coming to the House of Hope a year ago, I never knew that God speaks to His people. At first the idea, to me, seemed a little far-fetched. If God did speak, I figured He'd do it to people that either knew Him better than I did or that were walking more closely with Him. Little did I know that He longs to speak to ME always meeting me right where I am. Journaling didn't come easy for me. It took me a while to grasp—not only because of my unbelief, but because I was half expecting Him to speak to me in some audible, powerful, or emotional way. I wish I could have read Janet's book during this time to show me that God speaks to us in a still small voice—as she says, "through the eyes of our heart."

Journaling has really helped me this year, not

only to overcome drugs and alcohol, but to find my identity in Him. I love how Janet takes her real (and very personal!) issues to the Creator of the Universe and allows Him to minister to her as only He can. It shows the very nature of His character—a loving Father who is deeply concerned over even the tiniest of details in the lives of His children. I highly recommend this book to anyone who has never previously known that God still speaks to us today, or to anyone who longs to experience Him in a deeper, more intimate way. I encourage you to read along one day at a time and see how journaling can transform your life—and you!!!

Nicole Schreiber

I have known Janet and Jim Gilham for over 15 years. I have known both to be genuine "God Chasers." Janet reintroduced me to Mark and Patti Virkler when she gave me their book, *Dialogue with God*. Not only did it reawaken my prayer life through journaling, but so affected those around us that we went through two cases of the books in our New Covenant Church congregation. Janet served for years as an intercessory prayer partner of mine in an Inner Healing Prayer Ministry. She now ministers with several of the women mentioned in this book. I am amazed how much "Janet" there is on these pages. To read this is to know her. Read and be inspired.

Jimmy D. Smith
Author of *Imagine That*
Retired Associate Pastor
New Covenant Church, Valdosta, Georgia

Intimacy with God through Journaling is a book that will show you how to commune with God on a more personal level. If you're like me, always looking for a better way to hear from God, this will be an answer for you. Throughout my life, my way of journaling was to write down a scripture that the Lord highlighted for me, or to write down specific things He would show me throughout the day. After reading Janet's book and trying this method of two-way journaling, I have come to a place of having more of a conversation with God, like you would with a friend.

This book is a perfect example of how you can hear from God about the smallest to the largest details of your life. Janet shows her own personal experience of God's faithfulness as she takes her daily struggles, as well as her dreams and desires, to Him. I walked with her during much of what she shares in this book, and I witnessed that these times spent with the Lord brought truth and comfort to her. Just being able to get in His presence will connect you to an encounter with God that will change your life! Just be receptive and attentive, and you can hear His voice.

Gwen Turner

Acknowledgements

To the Holy Spirit: Thank You for guiding me, comforting me, teaching me and always being ready to speak to me when I still myself and wait on You.

To Mark Virkler: Thank you for your encouragement and counsel in putting my journaling into a book. It amazes me how, in your busy schedule, you always take the time to stop and answer any questions I have, or direct me to the right resources. One thing that blesses me so much is seeing your sincere desire to let people know that God will speak to them. Though you have been doing this for years, it's obvious that it's not just business as usual for you—it's your passion.

To Nicole Schreiber: Thank you for giving up hours of your free time to edit my book. You went above and beyond what I could have asked. You truly put your heart into it, and I appreciate you so much for that.

To Carol Barker and Gwen Turner, my prayer partners and very dear friends: Thank you for faithfully praying for me and encouraging me throughout the process of putting this book together and getting it published. I can always count on your prayers; they are priceless to me.

To my husband, Jimmy: Thank you for always

being willing to read or listen to my journaling and sharing with me what the Lord says to you about it. Thank you, also, for encouraging me that I do hear the voice of God during times that I have had questions.

To Jimmy Smith: You have been a spiritual father and friend to me. Thank you for taking the time to read my manuscript—making corrections and giving me godly advice.

To the ladies at the House of Hope: Thank you for be so willing to share your own personal experiences with journaling, to be included in this book. Knowing each of you and watching you grow in the Lord has been such a blessing in my life.

To Jami Duncan: Thank you for gathering all the ladies' journaling together, voluntarily typing them up for me and always being there to help in any way.

Table of Contents

Foreword xiii

Introduction xv

Day 1 • August 10, 2005 1

Day 2 • April 19, 2006 3

Day 3 • December 22, 2007 7

Day 4 • October 1, 2009 9

Day 5 • July 14, 2011 17

Day 6 • July 16, 2011 21

Day 7 • July 28, 2011 25

Day 8 • August 10, 2011 27

Day 9 • August 20, 2011 31

Day 10 • September 6, 2011 35

Day 11 • September 12, 2011 39

Day 12 • October 10, 2011 45

Day 13 • October 17, 2011 51

Day 14 • December 22, 2011 57

Day 15 • January 18, 2012 63

Day 16 • February 15, 2012 67

Day 17 • March 16, 2012 71

Day 18 • April 9, 2012 75

Day 19 • May 7, 2012.................................... 79

Day 20 • June 1, 2012.................................... 83

Day 21 • July 15, 2012 87

Day 22 • August 25, 2012 93

Day 23 • September 15, 2012........................ 97

Day 24 • November 2, 2012 99

Day 25 • February 20, 2013.........................103

Day 26 • June 2, 2013..................................111

Day 27 • July 30, 2013 117

Day 28 • August 31, 2013 119

Appendix A • The House of Hope 121

Appendix B • You Can Hear God's Voice..133

Prayer of Salvation 141

My Prayer for You 143

About the Author 145

Foreword

It is such a thrill and honor to write a foreword for *Intimacy with God through Journaling* by Janet Gilham. Janet has learned how to have a close relationship with God. She can hear His voice and see Him. She does this through two-way journaling, which she includes as a part of her devotional times. This is remarkable because, in the early days of our Christian walk, neither Janet nor I knew how to hear God's voice.

In the Bible we can read examples of people hearing God's voice. There even a book published in the 1980's titled *God Calling* by Two Listeners, in which the writers were hearing God's voice and writing down what He was speaking. It is interesting to me that, at the time the book was published, it was so uncommon to hear God's voice clearly through two-way journaling that the writers of the book would not even attach their names to it. The intent of the book "God Calling" was not to train others to hear God's voice, but simply to share a series of journaling's where two listeners had heard Gods voice. So that made me extremely hungry to hear God's voice, but left me wondering, "How do you do this?"

So I just hungered to hear, just as Janet did, along with so many other Christians today. Well, finally

God has provided a series of clear steps that we can take to easily hear His voice on a daily basis, and Janet describes the four steps in the first couple pages of this book. She took these steps herself and now, she is presenting to you 28 inspiring days of two-way journaling where God is lovingly speaking to her heart.

So how about you go on this ride of *Intimacy with God through Journaling* with Janet, and experience the richness and wonder of God's voice as He speaks to Janet, and through her, to you? Then, why don't you try it yourself? We provide lots of free training materials on hearing God's voice on our website: www.CWGministries.org. We are thrilled to see an army rising up who can hear God's voice and who are releasing His creativity and healing love in ever so many ways. Thank you, Janet, for providing to us the wonderful gift of this book! We appreciate hearing what God has spoken to you and now, through you to us.

Dr. Mark Virkler
Author of *4 Keys To Hearing God's Voice*

Introduction

My sheep hear My voice, and I know them, and they follow Me. John 10:27

In January, of 2005, my husband had an experience with the Lord that lasted approximately two weeks. He was literally in the presence of God the entire time, with the exception of a little rest now and then. The Lord was speaking to him often—throughout the day and into the night. Throughout that two week period, the Lord loved, encouraged and corrected him as he basked in His presence.

I became so hungry to experience what my husband was experiencing. I remember one day going desperately to God and telling him that I wanted to hear His voice like my husband was hearing it. For years I would "journal" my thoughts and prayers to God, but it was all one-sided. I talked to God, but I didn't know how to hear him talk back to me.

Later that year a friend shared a book with me titled, *How to Hear the Voice of God in a Noisy World* by Teresa Seputis. It was eye opening for me. I learned, for the first time, ways that God had already been speaking to me. I also learned that, through journaling, I could ask God things, and He would actually answer me. Thus I began two-way journaling.

Soon after that, I purchased *Dialogue with God* by Mark and Patti Virkler. I devoured the book and began journaling according to the 4 step process taught in their book. This took me to another level in my journaling. I shared it with one of my pastors. He got the book and began journaling himself. He was so changed by it that he bought several copies and began giving one to everyone he counseled.

One thing that I identified with in *Dialogue with God* was how our minds will wander and ask questions like, "God, was that You, or was it me or was it the devil?" I found that when I write following spontaneity, just flowing with what I am hearing, I don't have time to ask all those questions. Do I ever get it wrong? Is it ever me or the devil? Absolutely, but I do what Mark and Patti teach. I go with the flow and judge it later to see that it lines up with the Word of God. Also, as they teach, if I have questions or if it is something life changing, I will go to two or three witnesses to receive confirmation.

Journaling using the steps taught in their book has changed my life. The four steps (stillness, vision, spontaneity and writing) have been a vital key to my going deeper in communion with God. Getting still before God was the hardest for me. When I got alone with the Lord, I always felt like I needed to be doing something—praying, praising or just talking to Him. But each step in the process helps me with the next one. Getting still (step 1) helps me to get my focus on Jesus (Step 2). It doesn't take long for the spontaneity to come (step 3), and then I begin writing (step 4).

You may be a Christian who loves the Lord but, like me, you didn't realize that He would speak directly to you. I have compiled 28 days of my personal journaling, over a span of several years, to share with you. My prayer is that you will be encouraged to try the four step method from *Dialogue with God* and get started with your own intimate communion with God.

As you read these pages, I suggest that you read only one day at a time. Then stop, close your eyes, and focus on Jesus—His goodness, His character and all that He is. A particular Bible story may come to mind. Be still and watch for what the Lord may want to say to you. Write it down. When you have done this for 28 days you will have a compilation of your own personal communion with God. May the Lord bless you in your journey to hear His voice.

Day 1

August 10, 2005

Good morning, Father. Good morning, Jesus. Good morning, Holy Spirit. I praise You this morning. I worship You, and I seek You this morning. Holy Spirit, come into my prayer time, and speak to me. Show me how to pray and what to pray. Anoint me, Father, with Your Holy Spirit. Jesus, show me how to be more like You. Father, forgive me for my sins. Forgive me for my anger and judgment. By Your grace, I confess it as sin, and I repent. I choose to walk in love, mercy, and compassion; and not in anger and judgment. Lord, I need You. Take me to the places where there are still wounds in me, so that I will not be afraid to be all You want me to be. Lord, I thank You for my husband and for his leadership and counsel. And I thank You for teaching me to submit to his authority. I love it when You speak to me through him. You are awesome, Lord. Forgive me for having so much focus on the problem and not on You. Thank You for

Your correction through Jimmy. Please help me to get my focus back on You and to put my problems in Your hands.

Lord, what do You want to say to me today?

"Janet, My child, you are concerned about many things. There is only one thing to be concerned with and that is keeping your focus on Me. As you do this, all the other concerns will fall into place. Seek Me first. You are right in taking your thoughts captive. Love, even in your thoughts. Come into My presence, and let Me fill you up. When you do that, you will be prepared for whatever arises in your day. You will be prepared for whatever satan throws at you. Seek Me, and you will find Me."

Oh, Lord, that is what I am trying to do right now. I really think it helps me to type or write my prayers because it shuts out the other thoughts. I just want to be with You, Lord. I need some peace. I seem to be reacting to everything. Please give me Your peace.

"My peace I give to you. Receive it. Go and meet your husband. We'll chat along the way. I love you."

.

Day 2

April 19, 2006

Lord, What do you want to say to me this morning? Speak to me through the eyes of my heart.

(I see a picture of Jesus with children all around Him, and I'm there. I am a little bit far away. He tells me to come closer.)

"Come in closer, child. Don't be afraid. Come closer to Me. I am your Shepherd, and you are one of My Sheep. I will care for you. Come over closer to Me."

(Next, I see myself as a child, coming up to where the other children are.)

"Come even closer, child. Come into My lap. It's big enough for you."

(It seems that I have a hard time coming up into His lap.)

"Don't be afraid, My child."

(Then He picks me up and puts me in His lap. Now I am in His lap, but sitting kind of stiff. He's trying to pull me closer, but I'm kind of resistant.)

"Come closer, My child. There's nothing to be afraid of. Let Me comfort you. Let Me love you."

(With hesitation and maybe some fear, I lean against Him. It feels good, but I'm not sure about being this close. So I am sitting up again, and He's letting me. Now He's stroking my hair.)

What is this all about, Lord? What do You want to say to me through this vision?

(I'm now seeing a vision I've seen before where Jesus and I are playing on the beach. We're holding hands, then lying on the sand talking and kind of playing like children play.)

"Janet, you come to Me, and you will let Me get a little closer to you. But then there is a stopping place. You only let Me get so close, and then you back off. I want you to come closer. It's OK to come closer to Me. It's a safe place. It may seem scary to you, but it is the safest place you can be. I want you to come into My arms, and let Me just love you. As you come into My arms and just let Me love you, you will become full of My love and be able to give it to others. Come child. Come in closer. Let Me shower you with My love."

April 19, 2006

Why would You want to do that, Lord? I am not worthy of that kind of love.

"You are Mine, and I am yours. I love you, child, and I want you to feel My love like you never have before."

Well, how do I do that exactly, Lord?

"Just do it. Come closer. Go back to the vision and come closer into My arms."

I'm afraid that I'm only going to get to watch it, like it's someone else. I'm afraid that I won't be able to feel it.

"Don't be afraid. Perfect love casts out fear, and My love is perfect. Come. I want you to come into My presence every day and just let Me love you. That is where you are changed. Now go and listen for My voice as you listen to Isaiah, and don't feel like you have to do the entire book. Listen for a while, then go and minister to your husband. Remember child, I love you. You are precious to Me."

Thank You, Lord.

"You're welcome. Come back soon to this place."

Day 3

December 22, 2007

Good morning, Lord. It is very early for me to be up. I don't know why I couldn't sleep, but here I am. I have enjoyed reading Your Word this morning. Your Word is a lamp unto my feet and a light unto my path. Thank you for Your Word. I love You, Lord. I love You, Father. I love You with all my heart, all my soul, all my strength, and all my mind. You are my God in whom I trust, and I praise You. I love You, Jesus, and I love You, Holy Spirit. Speak to me this morning, Lord. I know I am not up this early for no reason at all. What would You like to say to me this morning?

"Thank you, child, for choosing Me first this morning. I know you were tempted to go straight to work on your calendars, but you didn't, and I appreciate that. You will have time to do all you have to do—and more. I will give you back the time you give Me—and more. I will give you the rest you need.

Don't let the cares of this world get you overwhelmed. I am with you always, even to the ends of the earth. You don't have to be anxious for anything, but in everything by prayer and petition, with thanksgiving, make your requests known to Me. I am here for you always. The steps of the righteous are ordered. I shall order your steps in the next few days so that you get done what needs to be done without being anxious. Choose not to be anxious. Choose peace. Remember what this season is all about. Stop and ponder My birth. Meditate on it. Meditate on the events that took place surrounding My birth. Read the Christmas book and ponder what is in it. Enjoy this time. Don't wish it away. Instead of getting into the calendars now, go back to bed and rest. You will be able to get them done later. I love you, child. Thank you again for choosing Me this morning."

Thank You, Lord. Amen.

Day 4

October 1, 2009

Hello, Lord.

"Hello, child."

Lord, It's already October 1st. Wow! This year has gone by fast. It seems that the years are going by faster and faster. Lord, it's 1:15 in the morning, and I couldn't sleep; so I decided to spend some time with You. I have been reading Your Word. What a blessing it is! I love Your Word, Lord. I love You. You are so wonderful and so kind. Thank You for loving me so much. You are absolutely the best of the best. Thank You for always being here for me. I know that You are with me always. That brings me so much comfort. Thank You for saving me. I am so glad that I get to know You. Thank You for teaching me how to recognize Your voice. I am so glad to be one of your sheep, Lord. You are my Savior, my King, my Lord and my Healer. You are my Friend, my Father and my Redeemer. You are my Rock, my

Counselor and my God in whom I trust. You are mine, and I am Yours. What a wonderful revelation! I am Yours. Wow! Thank You for loving me so much. Thank You for all the many blessings You have bestowed upon me. Thank You for Jimmy, Melody, Scott, Mia, Ella, Sam, Alex, Nancy, Todd, Emma Grace and Noah. Thank You for all my extended family. Thank You for all my friends. You have blessed me with so many godly friends. Thank You so much for that. Thank You for my home and for our camper. Thank You for my marriage. Thank You for wisdom and revelation. Thank You for speaking to me. Thank You for knowledge and understanding. Thank You for loving me so much. I always feel Your love, and I always know You're there for me. It seems that no matter how bad things get, I always know Your love. Thank You so much for that. Lord, I desire to be in Your presence. I would love to sing right now but I don't want to wake up Jimmy. The song I would sing if I could right now is this: You are so beautiful to me. You're everything I hope for. You're everything I need.

Speak to me this morning, Lord, through the eyes of my heart. What do You want to say to me right now?

(I see the Lord hugging me and swinging me around like I'm a little child.)

October 1, 2009

"I love you, little one. You are precious to Me. I love to be with you. I love for you to come into My presence. Stay with Me a while, child, and sup with Me."

(I see the Lord setting out a meal, like maybe a picnic meal.)

"Let's spend some time together, child."

Here I am, Lord. I'm here.

"I'm here too."

Lord, what do You want to say to me?

"Child, there are so many things I want to say to you. I want to say that you are beautiful to Me, and that you are everything I hoped for when I created you. I knit you together in your mother's womb. I knew you then. I have always known you. I know your every thought. I know your lying down and you waking up. I am with you always, even to the end of the earth. You are never alone. You never have any reason to fear. I am pleased that you are fearing less and less. I am pleased by your heart towards Me and My statutes. Your heart is pure, and that is what I am looking at always—your heart. Keep it pure before Me. Don't let junk into your heart."

Lord, forgive me for the ugly words that came out of my mouth today when I got hurt. I hate that those words are in my heart. Would You take them from me? I pray that I will never need to say words like that again and that no matter what happens, only good words come out of me. Change my heart to be like Yours, Lord.

"I am, child. Your heart is changing and getting purer and purer. There was a time when you would not have been convicted by the words you used. I am pleased that bothered you."

Lord, I want to be all that You want me to be.

"Child, don't strive so hard. Let My grace be sufficient enough for you. I am with you, and My grace is truly sufficient for you."

Lord, a few weeks ago, You told me to turn my eating and weight over to You, and I believe I did. For a couple of weeks, I could see Your grace at work. I wasn't desiring extra food or even sodas. But something has changed, and it's hard again. I'm struggling again, and I've been overeating. What has happened?

"You have taken back control."

In what way have I taken back control?

"One way is by weighing yourself often. Your focus is still on your weight. Let it go. Let the weight go. Give it to Me."

Can I ever weigh?

October 1, 2009

"How about weigh only once a month for a while?"

Today is the first. Can I weigh myself today?

"You may. Then don't weigh yourself again until the first of next month."

Ok, Lord, I will do that. Help me.

"I will."

What else am I doing wrong?

"You are still struggling. Stop the struggle."

I don't know how to stop struggling. Help me, Lord.

"I am. Give your eating to Me every day. Every time you think about your weight and every time you think about eating, just hand it over again and again until you have truly given Me this burden."

It has become a burden, hasn't it?

"Yes, very much so. Cast your burdens on Me. My yoke is easy and My burden is light. Cast all your cares on Me because I care for you. Remember My love for you, and you will know that I will take care of your every need."

Lord, change my heart about food and drink. Give me a desire for better things for my body.

"I am, but I don't want you to give any thought to

it. When you are hungry, eat. When you are thirsty, drink. Leave the rest to Me. Exercise, but don't get compulsive about that either. Give it all to Me. Let go, and let Me take care of this area of your life. I love you right where you are. Don't worry about what others might think of you. No one is thinking about your size like you are. You are already beautiful to Me, just as you are. Remember that."

Thank You, Lord.

"You don't have to thank Me for loving you. It's who I am. There is nothing hard about it. I love you with an everlasting love, and I love with an ultimate, unconditional love—no strings attached. I already love you as much as I can love you; you don't have to do anything else. No matter what you do, My love for you never changes. Did you know that?"

Yes, I know that. It's hard to comprehend sometimes, but it's nice to hear it. Lord, help me to really internalize the love You have for me.

"I am. No matter what you do, good or bad, My love for you never changes. If you get angry, I love you. If you give away all you have, I love you the same. My love for you is constant, never changing and complete. There's no greater love than the love I have for you. I don't love a single person more than I love you. I love you the best that I love. If you are rude, I don't love you any less; if you are kind, I

don't love you anymore. Yes, some things you do please Me more than others, but nothing you do changes the depth of My love for you."

Wow, Lord! That is good to know. NO, that is GREAT to know! Help me know it in every part of my being.

"Janet, if you eat 'right', I love you; and if you overeat, I love you. If you drink water, I love you. If you drink soda, I love you. Do you get My point?"

I think I do, Lord. Thank You for loving me.

"My pleasure. Loving you is not difficult for Me, and it is not difficult for others either. People love you, Janet. You are a very lovable person."

Why?

"Maybe they see Me in you. And I AM love."

I hope so. I really hope so. That's what I want people to see when they see me.

"They do."

Oh, Lord, I'm afraid that I may be keeping Jimmy awake with all this typing. I could stay in Your presence all night. Sleep doesn't seem to matter when I am with You.

"I will give you rest. But it's OK for you to go back to bed. I will be with you. If you are awake, you can continue to talk to Me in your thoughts; and I

will talk to you, also, until you fall asleep."

Thank You, Lord. You are so wonderful!

"You are too, child."

I love You. Thanks for this time together. Thanks for taking what the enemy meant for harm and turning it to good.

"You are welcome. Now go back to bed; I will give you rest."

.

Day 5

July 14, 2011

Good evening, my precious Lord Jesus. I hope You have had a blessed day.

"I have, and I bless you, child. Thank you for coming to be with Me. I love for you to come into My presence. I love to speak to you. I love to share My secrets with My people. I want to share more with you."

Lord, I love when You share with me. I love to hear Your voice. Thank You for letting me have an intimate relationship with You. I pray for even more intimacy with You. I pray for the supernatural to be natural in Jimmy's and my life. Pour out Your Spirit on us so that we can accomplish all that You have for us to do here. We need Your Holy Spirit poured out on us to be all that You want us to be and to do all that You want us to do. Lord, we're hungry for Your presence. Like the man shared on the program today; I want to hunger more for You. I want my hunger to be filled with You. Fill me, Lord. Fill Jimmy. Fill us to overflowing with Your presence so that we may do the things that You did and even greater things, by Your power. Send Your power, Lord. I pray for a move of Your Holy Spirit in our church like the Brownsville revival. I pray for an anointing on our pastor like he has never seen. Pour out Your Spirit on him and on our church so that we can minister to this city like never before. Let Your Spirit flow in all of our services. Bless our church so that we may be a blessing to this city and the surrounding cities. Help us to bring redemption to this area. Help us to bring healing and deliverance. Lord, we are known as the "Bible Belt." Show Your power in the Bible Belt so that we might live up to all that name could mean.

Holy Spirit, have Your way in Jimmy and me. Do whatever You want to do in us. Cleanse us and purify us of all unrighteousness. Pour out Your love in our hearts so that we may give Your love to others. Fill me. Fill us. Change us to be all that You would have us be. Let the giftings that You have deposited in us, in our children, and in our grandchildren come to fruition. Let our gifts flow out to minister to others. Lord, I am desperate for You. I am desperate for Your presence. I am desperate for Your power. Don't let me be disappointed. Fill me up, Lord. Change me, Use me. Let me be Your hands and feet.

Lord, what do You want to say to me tonight?

July 14, 2011

"Your desires are My desires. I am giving you the desires of your heart. You will touch the lives of many more people in the remainder of your lifetime on this earth. You have already touched more lives than you realize, but that number will increase greatly and multiply to multitudes. I am going to use you and Jimmy in mighty ways. You are going to do greater things than even I did while I was on the earth. You are going to be filled. Supernatural is going to be the norm for you and Jimmy. I am doing a new thing. Do you not perceive it? I am making a way in the desert, and new things are coming. Child, only believe, and stay close to Me and My Word. Pray in the Spirit on all occasions, and you will see My glory. You will see My power in ways that most have never even dreamed of. You will experience My power in ways that most never do. You will be right in the middle of My next great move, just as you have desired.

Your eyes are healed, child. Jimmy's pain is healed. He is delivered from smoking. You are delivered from overeating. You are free. He is free. His youth is renewed like the eagles. His lungs are clear, clean, and healthy. His heart is healthy. He is the healed of God. You are the healed of God. Receive your healing. Bless and do not curse. Speak life, not death and curses. Speak only blessings. I love you, child. Never forget My love for you. And never forget My power. Walk close to Me. Now go rest, knowing that I am with you always. I will never leave you or forsake you

Thank You, Lord. Amen.

Day 6

July 16, 2011

Hello, Holy Spirit.

"Hello, precious one."

Lord, teach me to know You better as the Person of the Holy Spirit. Draw me closer to You. Give me a deep, deep hunger to get closer to You. I already have a hunger to get closer to You, but I want more. I want more, and more, and more of You, Holy Spirit. There is a reason that I have always longed to be in places where Your Holy Spirit is present and where miracles are taking place. I know that I am supposed to be in some type of healing ministry and, in fact, I am. But I want more. I want more of You, Holy Spirit. I want to know Your voice better. I want to sense Your presence more. I want to feel Your presence. I want to know Your love on a much, much deeper level so that I can pass it on to others. Draw me nearer, Holy Spirit. Teach me Your ways; tell me Your dreams and desires. I want to know Your heart. Show me Your heart. Show me what You want from me. Tell me about You. Speak to me, Holy Spirit, like I've never known before. Here I am, Lord.

"And here I am, child. I see your heart. I am passionate about you. I so desire to draw you in closer. I am so pleased that you desire the same. Come, child. Come closer. Come out into the deep with Me."

(I see Jesus taking me out into deep water.)

"Don't be afraid, child. I am with you always. Much can happen out in the deep. Greater things than you have ever seen can happen in the deep. Come, child. Do not fear."

Here I am, Lord.

"Here I AM, child."

What do we do now, Lord?

"We wait."

We wait?

"Yes, those that hunger and thirst for righteousness shall be filled."

Lord, thank You for that word. I do hunger and thirst for righteousness. I want to be filled.

"Those who wait upon the Lord shall renew their strength. I will pour out My Spirit on you and you

July 16, 2011

will prophesy, you will dream dreams, and you will see visions. You will lay hands on the sick, and they will recover. You will set the captives free. You will heal the brokenhearted, cleanse the lepers, and raise the dead. You will walk in the gifts of My Spirit at My choosing. You will walk in all the gifts at My choosing. I am anointing you to do My work. My Spirit is with you always. You, by My Spirit, will do mighty works. Child, I love the way you love Me and want to please Me. You delight yourself in Me, and I am giving you the desires of your heart."

Well, my number one desire right now is to be closer to You; to know Your presence in a deeper way and to feel Your presence like never before.

"I know. That's why it is so easy to give you more because you desire the right things."

Lord, I desire You. I desire a relationship with You, Holy Spirit—a living, daily communication with You. I know that we already have a relationship, but I want more. I want the manifestation of Your presence in my life. Is it wrong to want that?

"No, it is right to want that."

Lord, I want to know You like Kathryn Kuhlman knew You. I want to know You as my Friend and Companion like she did. I want You, Holy Spirit, to be more real to me than anything else, just like her.

"You will; I am no respecter of persons."

Right now, I am really hungering for Your presence. I want to crave being with You like I have craved food. I want You, Holy Spirit. I want You to teach me all things. Teach me to walk in Your ways. Teach me to hear Your voice more clearly. Give me a deeper hunger and a deeper faith. I pray for the gift of faith to rise up in me.

"Just wait, child. Wait. I'm here with you."

Lord, if my motives are wrong, change my motives. I want to know You more. Change me, Lord; however You desire to change me. I'm Yours. Have Your way in me.

"Go to My Word, child."

Where, Lord?

"Hebrews."

Where in Hebrews?

"Chapter 9".

Day 7

July 28, 2011

Good morning, my sweet Lord.

"Good morning, My child."

Lord, I praise You, I honor You, and I bless You. You are so wonderful and so kind. You are my God in whom I trust. I love You so much. Thank You for loving me so much. Thank You for always being there for me. I bless You, Lord. I honor and adore You. I love You with all my heart, all my mind, all my strength, and all my soul. Thank You for blessing me so that I might be a blessing to others. Show me ways to bless others while we are on this trip. I pray for Your anointing on me and on Jimmy to be a blessing everywhere we go, particularly this weekend to our grandchildren and Emily. Thank You for Emily and for her being able to go with us. Let us bless her these three days. Lord, I thank You for Your protection ahead of time, for all of these children, and for us as we spend a lot of time in the water, in the sun and camping. I thank You for this time to rest, relax and have fun. You are such a wonderful God. Thank You for letting me know You. Lord, I want to know You more, and I want to know more about how Your Kingdom works. Thank You for giving me revelation from the Scripture this morning so quickly after I asked. I love You so much. I desire Your presence in my life always. I thank You that You are always with me. Lord, I desire to know what You have to say to me this morning. Speak to me through the eyes of my heart.

"Be still, and know that I am always with you. Do not fear. Do not let fear at any level come upon you. Stand firm. Take authority over your environment. Take authority over your family. You have the power to make a difference because My power is in you. Bind up what needs to be bound up, and loose what needs to be loosed. Have fun on your trip, but always be aware of the enemy's schemes. Pray in the Spirit often, and I will be praying through you the things that you cannot see. Now go and help your husband. Remember to love him. Don't react to him. Love him."

I will, Lord. Thank You!

Day 8

August 10, 2011

Good morning, my precious Lord.

"Good morning, My child."

Lord, I praise You. Lord, I honor You, and I bless You. I adore You, Jesus. I exalt You, and I extol You. You are my God in whom I trust. You are my Healer. You are my Great Physician. You are my King and my Lord. You are my Father God; my Abba Father. You are my Jesus. You are my Holy Spirit. I am one with You, and You are one with me. We are one just as You and the Father are One. Am I correct?

"You are."

Jesus, speak to me this morning through the eyes of my heart. I will be still and watch to see what You have to say to me.

(I see miracles. I see Jesus and the girl who touched the hem of His garment. *"Your faith has made You whole,"* Jesus said. I see Jesus healing the blind man. I see Him making mud and putting it on his eyes. I see the man from the movie shouting. "I can see! I can see!" I see Jesus touching someone's legs and them being healed. I see Jesus touching ears and them being healed. I see Jesus casting out a demon.)

Lord, why are all these miracles coming to mind?

"I want you to know that you will see greater things than these. You will do even greater things than these."

Will I, Lord? That is my desire. I want to walk in the supernatural.

"You will. That is My desire also. Draw near to Me, and I will draw near to you. The closer you get to Me, the closer you will get to My power."

Lord, how do I draw nearer to You?

"By doing just what you are doing; praying in the Spirit, setting aside time to be with Me, and by just focusing on Me. Also by reading My Word and letting it soak into your spirit. Let My words come alive in your spirit. As they come alive, I will come alive in your spirit like never before."

Lord, fill me up to overflowing with Your rivers of living water.

"I am. Come close."

August 10, 2011

Lord, I want more of You.

"I have more to give you. Come close."

Lord, I pray that as I read Your words every day that they would come alive in me like never before. Fill me with Your Word.

"I am. Stay close."

Lord, I feel like the author felt in the book I just read. He said, "If I can't be in Your presence here on earth, why be here?" I need You, Lord. I need Your presence desperately.

"Yes, you do, and you can have it any time you desire."

I can?

"You can."

Show me how.

"I have. Walk in what I have already shown you."

Do You mean read the Bible, pray in the Spirit, praise, worship, and come into Your presence?

"That is exactly what I mean. The more you do these things, the more you will be filled."

Lord, help me to hunger and thirst for Your Word and for Your presence even more.

"I am. Come close."

Lord, I am here. I am with You.

"And I am with you, child."

Lord, I praise You, and I love You so very much. You are so wonderful to me. You are so kind and so precious to me. Thank You for my prayer language. Teach me to sing in the Spirit.

"You can sing in the Spirit any time you desire."

Lord, expand my prayer language. I desire a beautiful heavenly language.

"You have it, child. You have a heavenly language. Pray in it often."

I do.

"Yes, you do. Pray in it even more. Pray in the Spirit on all occasions."

Lord, what about these petitions we are learning about? Will You help me make my petitions?

"You know I will. Make them, and print them. Put them in a folder, and keep them so that you can go back and see what I have already done."

Lord, I am going to start a new document and write out some things to make a petition for.

"I'll be right here with you."

Thank You, Lord.

"My pleasure."

Day 9

August 20, 2011

Thank You, Lord, for Your Word. I pray that it would get deeply rooted in me, in Jimmy, and in our children and grandchildren. Help each of us to hunger and thirst for Your Word. Lord, You are so wonderful and so kind. Thank You for the opportunity to share Your Word, particularly Psalm 91, at the school. Lord, during Chapel time, give me the ways to present it to each age group so that it will have a great impact on their lives. I pray for wisdom and discernment as I study and prepare to teach it to the kids. Lord, I praise You, I honor You, and I bless You. You are my refuge and my fortress, my God in whom I trust. I do trust You, Lord. Thank You for always being with me. Holy Spirit, guide me into all truth, and spread the love of God in my heart so that I may walk in that love every day of my life. Forgive me, Lord, and forgive Jimmy, too, for our grumbling and complaining. Help us to walk in an attitude of thankfulness and gratitude, not even mentioning the things that aren't going well. Lord, put a guard over our mouths, and help us to not speak against Your Word in any way. Help us to only speak that which lines up with Your Word. Lord, make us like You in every way. You said You made us in Your image. Help us to walk in that image more and more. I want more of You, Jesus, and less of me. I want all of You and none of me. That is my desire. Cleanse Jimmy and me, and purify us of all unrighteousness. Help us to walk in love everywhere we go.

Lord, are there some things that You would like to say to me this morning? Speak to me through the eyes of my heart.

(I see Jesus riding with us to Tallahassee and enjoying being with us.)

"Let's go and have a good time. I will be with you. Don't be afraid. Child; remember how precious you are to Me and how precious your family is to Me. I will protect you on the road and in your travels. I will be with you always. It's true that when you show up the Kingdom shows up."

(Now, I see Him working in the yard alongside Jimmy.)

"I am with him always. Continue to pray for him, believing for his total healing and deliverance. Don't listen to the lies of the enemy. He is trying to trip you up. You have recognized this; now act on it. Don't

August 20, 2011

ponder the thoughts he puts in your head; resist them. Resist him, and he has to flee. Declare My Word over Jimmy every day. Speak life into your situation every day. Speak life into Jimmy every day. Don't speak curses. Don't entertain curses or lies from satan. That's what he wants you to do, so that you can come to believe him instead of My Word. Don't listen. Don't even give him the time of day. Take your thoughts captive, replacing his thoughts with My Word. You know how to do this. Walk in My ways, and he can't do a thing to you. Remember Psalm 91 for yourself, as well as those you pray for. Stand firm on what My Word says. Let it be the final say so in everything that concerns you and those you love. My Word is powerful and sharper than a double-edged sword. Remember the power in My Word. Use it often; read or listen to it daily. Meditate on it day and night, so that it goes deep inside you—so that it abides in you. Let My Word abide in you. It's ok to play some, but don't let playing games take the place of spending time in My Word. It is life to you and to those you pray for. Child, I am very pleased with you. Stay close, and you will do great things for My Kingdom. Come into My presence often, and we will sup together. Then you will be able to walk in My power and do greater things than I was able to do while I was on earth. You have much more time than I did while I was there."

Lord, give me boldness to share Your message

with those who don't know You.

"I am. Your boldness is growing and will continue to grow. Fear not, for I am always with you, and I will always give you the words you need to say. Trust Me and My power at work in you. Don't trust yourself. Trust Me. In My power, you can do anything. I will enable you to do all that I have put you here to do. Just lean on and trust in Me."

I trust You, Lord. Show me how to trust You more.

"I am. Stay close to My Word. It will give you boldness the more you read and meditate on it. It will grow in you like a flourishing tree, and it will sprout. It will have to. You won't be able to contain it. It will have to come out because it will be who you are. Now go and prepare for your day. You will have time to rest. I love you, precious child. Know that."

I do know that, Lord. Your love for me means so much to me. Thank You for loving me so much, and for enabling me to know it. I love You, Lord. I love You more than anything.

"I know."Thank you for this time together.

Thank you, Lord. Have a blessed day, Lord.

"And You do the same."

Day 10

September 6, 2011

Good morning, my Lord.

"Good morning, precious one."

Lord, I bless You this morning. I praise You and I honor You, Jesus. You are my God in whom I trust. You are my refuge and my fortress. You are my King and my Lord. Bless You, Lord. I love You, Father, with all my heart, all my mind, all my strength, and all my soul. I adore You, Father. Holy Spirit, I adore You. Thank You for comforting me and for guiding me into all truth. Thank You for filling me up to overflowing with Your presence. Bless me, Lord, that I might be a blessing to others. Bless me indeed. Enlarge my territory. Let Your hand be upon me and keep me from evil. Lord, I pray for Jimmy. I thank You that he dwells in the secret place of the Most High and abides under the shadow of the Almighty. He says of You that You are his refuge and his fortress, his God in whom he trusts. Surely You shall deliver him from the snare of the fowler and from the deadly pestilence. You cover him with Your feathers, and under Your wings Jimmy takes refuge. Jimmy shall not fear the terror by night, nor the arrow that flies by day, nor the pestilence that stalks in the darkness, nor the destruction that lays waste at noonday. A thousand may fall at Jimmy's side, ten thousand at his right hand, but it will not come near him. Only with his eyes shall he look and see the reward of the wicked. Because he has made the Lord his refuge and the Most High his dwelling place, no evil shall befall him, nor shall any plague come near his dwelling. For You give Your angels charge over him, and keep him in all his ways. In their hands they bear him up, lest he dash his foot on a stone. He shall tread on the lion and the cobra; the young lion and the serpent he shall trample underfoot. Because he loves You, Lord, You will deliver him. You will set him on high because he has known Your name. When he calls on You, You will answer him. You will honor and deliver him. With long life will You satisfy Jimmy and show him Your salvation. Thank You, Lord, for Psalm 91 over my husband. Thank You for Your blood that covers him wherever he goes. Thank You for loving him so much. Thank You for delivering him from smoking. Thank You for prospering him. Thank You for downloading the book into his spirit and for enabling him to write all that You give him. Thank You for his book being a

September 6, 2011

best seller. I love You, Lord, and I want to bless You every day in some way.

"You do bless Me every day just by being you. You bless Me when you come to spend time with Me. You bless Me when you talk to Me. You are a blessing to Me, child. Always remember that; you are a great blessing to Me."

Thank You, Lord.

Is there anything else You want to say to me this morning?

"Stay on that course of blessing and not cursing. Bless every person and organization that comes before your eyes and ears. Bless, and do not curse. It is true that you put your own blessing on hold while you are cursing others. I release the blessing to you and Jimmy this day because you have repented of cursing others, and because you have chosen to bless instead of curse. That is a very wise decision, and I will help you to hold to it. If you fall, I will lift you back up. If you curse, repent and go back to blessing quickly. Blessing others will bring about your blessing more quickly. Watch your words. Make sure they are words that I would speak over someone and not words that satan would speak. Be in agreement with Me and My Word, not with satan and his words. That is where your blessing will come from. Always be thankful in every situation, if for nothing more

than that you know Me and know My love for you. Leave the lines open for blessing to come your way. Love and blessing is the answer to all your problems. Bless and pray for your debtors. Bless them with not only what you know that I would want for them, but also with what you would want Me to bless you. Speak life and not death into every person, organization and situation I put in your path, and your blessing will come forth a hundred-fold. Speak blessings over Jimmy, your children and children's children. Don't report the facts, speak blessing. Speak it over yourself also. Don't speak a bad report about yourself. Speak the blessing. I love you. Go now, and bless those I put in your path or in your thoughts today."

Thank You, Lord. I love You!

Day 11

September 12, 2011

Come, Holy Spirit, I need You. Speak to me. Show me how to commune with You. I love You, Holy Spirit. Thank You for comforting me, for communing with me, and for guiding me into all truth. Precious Holy Spirit, I don't want to go anywhere without You by my side. Have Your way in me. Guard my thoughts and my words. I pray that only the words of Jesus would come out of my mouth. Teach me about You, Holy Spirit. Teach me Your ways. Help me to know You better as a person, and help me to commune with You better.

"Child, I am with you always. I am the power behind all that you see the Father doing and all that you see Jesus doing. I come in power and in truth. I know all truth and all things, and I can teach you all things."

Then teach me, Holy Spirit. I want to learn from You every day. First of all teach me to come into

Your presence and stay in Your presence. Also teach me to walk in Your presence and live in Your presence. I desire Your presence wherever I am.

"I desire that too."

Holy Spirit, what grieves You?

"I am grieved when people don't recognize My power and My love for them. It is because of My love that My power is there for them. So when they don't recognize it or when they deny My power, it's because they don't know My love—the love of God the Father and God the Son."

Holy Spirit, I want to know Your power. I want to live in Your power, so that I am controlled by You and not by me. I want to be full of You, and walk in Your fullness. Show me how to do that.

"Come and spend time with Me daily. Come often throughout the day. You already commune with Me often, but come more and stay longer. Listen, because I am always speaking to you."

Teach me how to listen to Your voice better.

"I am."

Yes, I guess You are. Holy Spirit, You are welcome in my home, on my land and anywhere I go. I always want Your presence with me. Never leave me alone to my own resources. I am nothing without You.

September 12, 2011

"I am with you always."

Teach me Your ways. Teach me more about Jesus, and teach me more about My Father in Heaven. I want to know You more. I want to know everything about You, God. I want to be close to You, closer than ever. What do You want to teach me today, Holy Spirit?

"I want to teach you about the power and love of God. God loves you so much that He sent Jesus to die for you, so that your life would be a life of blessing and relationship with Him. He wants you to have abundant life. But He doesn't want you to squander it or not appreciate the abundance. He wants you to enjoy it, and pass it on to others. He wants to bless you because He loves you. Yes, He wants you to bless others, but He also wants to bless you simply because of His love for you and for no other reason."

More, Lord; teach me more.

"When Jesus died for you, it was for many things. He gave you peace, He gave you joy, He gave you salvation, and He gave you healing. Much was done on that cross for you; denying any of it is denying what He did for you. Those stripes were for your healing. He also died so that you could have power to trample on the enemy. That power comes from Me. I am the power behind the name of Jesus. You use the Name, and I send My power. That's how it works."

Wow! More, Lord, please teach me more.

"The Father speaks, 'Heal.' Jesus heals, and I am the power. When Jesus was on earth we were inseparable. He never went anywhere without Me. He was God, but He was man on the earth, and His power came from Me. He demonstrated what man can do in the power of His Name. You can do what He did on earth because I am here. I will show you what He wants you to do, and I will give you the power to do it."

That is my desire.

"That is the Father's and Jesus' desire also. They want you to walk in My fullness just as you have said you desire."

Teach me how, Holy Spirit.

"Dig into My Word. I will show you things in My Word that you have never seen before. I will reveal mysteries to you as you read. Invite Me in, every time you go to the Word."

Holy Spirit, I invite You in always, into every aspect of my life. I ask You now to come alongside me as I read the Word, and teach me new revelations. Come, Holy Spirit; I need You.

"Child, you know how powerful your sessions at the House of Hope have been?"

Yes, sir.

September 12, 2011

"It's because you always invite Me along. You put Me in charge and ask Me to have My way. That is why My power is there for you so often. Continue to invite Me in, and you will see more and more power in your sessions. Anytime you ask Me to come alongside you, I will. If you don't ask Me, I will keep silent."

Oh, Holy Spirit, You are invited into my life every minute of every day. Forgive me for the times I have done things in my own strength. Help me to always invite You in and to always listen for Your direction.

"I will, child. I will."

So it's You that I am truly communing with when I am journaling?

"It is, but is OK for you to speak to the Father and to Jesus. Just know it is I who is answering you because I am with you here on earth."

Sometimes I get confused as to whose name I am supposed to use.

"I know; but We are One, and there is no competition between us. God the Father gives the commands. Jesus follows His commands, and I give power to the command, just as Benny explains it in his book. But We are still one. And if sometimes you want to address Me as Father or as Jesus it's OK.

Just know that you are speaking to Me, Holy Spirit."

Holy Spirit, I want to know God as my Father better. As You know, I haven't had an earthly father for many years. He was a good father, but far from perfect. I want to know my perfect Father better. I want to know His love for me better. Will You teach me?

"I will. That's My job."

I want to go to Your Word, but I don't want to stop communing with You. I love to commune with You.

"I love it even more."

You sound like Patsy.

"I know. Actually, she sounds like Me."

She'd love to hear that.

"You can tell her I said that."

I will. Is it time for me to go to Your Word?

"You can go now. I will go with you."

Where should I read first?

"Galatians 5 & 6."

OK, I'll meet You there.

Day 12

October 10, 2011

Good morning, my precious Lord.

"Good morning, My precious one."

I love You, Father, with all my heart, all my mind, all my soul, and all my strength. You are my everything. You are my God in whom I trust. You are my Shield and my Buckler, my Deliverer and my Redeemer. You are Jesus. You are Holy Spirit. You are my Friend, my Father, my Brother and my Great Physician. Holy Spirit, You are my Guide and my Comforter. Guide me into all truth. Help me to rightly divide the Word. Help me to have new revelations as I read Your Word. Open up the Word to me in a whole new light. I pray for a spirit of wisdom and revelation, and of knowledge and understanding. I pray also for discernment. Lord, I bless You this morning. I honor You and I exalt You. You are everything to me. There is none like You; there is no one or nothing that even compares with You. I am nothing without You. I couldn't live without You. I need You every moment of every day by my side. Stay close, Lord. I thank You that You will never leave me nor forsake me, and that You are with me every moment of every day. I thank You that I can always count on Your love for me. I thank You for Your mercy and forgiveness. I thank You, Jesus, for going to the cross for me. I thank You for peace, for forgiveness of sins, for healing, for prosperity, and for preservation. I thank You for all that You have done for me and all that You provided for me on the cross. I love You so much. Help me to show my love to You more, and to be obedient to Your Word. Help me, Lord, to fulfill all that You have put me here to fulfill.

I pray for Jimmy, Lord. I pray for a fresh anointing on him. Thank You for blessing my husband, and for healing him. Thank You, Lord, for Jimmy. Thank You for his love for me. Thank You for loving me through him. I pray that You will pour out Your love on him in a fresh new way. I pray that he will feel Your love like never before. I pray that Your love will flow out of him to others like never before. I pray that wherever he and I go that Your love goes with us and through us to others. I pray that people feel Your presence whenever Jimmy and I are present. I thank You that when we show up the Kingdom shows up. I thank You that we are citizens

October 10, 2011

in Heaven and that we are just on assignment here. Lord, help us to complete those assignments to Your perfection.

Lord, I pray for our children and grandchildren. I pray Psalm 91 over them. Thank You that You give Your angels charge over them, and that no evil shall come near their homes. I thank You that when they call on You, You answer them. I thank You that they will each fulfill the assignments that You have put them on this earth to accomplish. I thank You for blessing them, Lord. Bless Scott, Melody, Mia, Ella, Alex and Sam. Bless Todd, Nancy, Emma Grace and Noah. Bless them with wonderful blessings, and a deeper knowledge of Your love. Bless their finances. Bless them to be a blessing to others.

Lord, speak to me this morning. Speak to me through the eyes of my heart. I will watch to see what You have to say to me.

(I just spent some time in spiritual warfare for my family. I've been walking around the living room praying and thanking God for what He has already done. I heard the Holy Spirit say, *"Now, that's prayer!"*)

Thank You, Holy Spirit, for teaching me how to pray.

"I will teach you more and more as you commune with Me. Stay close to Me and to My Word,

and you will see the spirit of wisdom and revelation, of knowledge and understanding, and of discernment come to life. Stay close, child. Stay close. Don't let work, play or anything else keep you from staying close. Get into My Word daily. I will meet you there and show you those new revelations you are asking for. I will show you the truth, and how to rightly divide My Word. There is a wealth of information and revelation for you there. I will open it up to you in ways you have never seen, if you will only go there."

Lord, forgive me for the times I've neglected to be in Your Word. Help me to not let a day go by without being in Your Word.

"Draw near to Me, and I will draw near to you."

Lord, I am desperate for You. Help me to stay focused on You and what Your Word says. Help me to not neglect time in Your Word or time alone with You. I love You so much, yet I let busyness and everything else get in the way of my spending time with You. Forgive me, Lord. I repent; I want to turn and become closer and closer to You. I want to know Your Word. Help me, as well as Jimmy and our family, to be deeply grounded and rooted in Your Word.

"I am, child."

Lord, is there anything else You want to say to me before I go to Your Word?

"I am here, child. We will go together, and I will speak to you there."

Is there a particular place You want me to go?

"Go to Hebrews."

Why Hebrews?

"You'll see. Come."

Day 13

October 17, 2011

I love You, Lord. I honor You and I bless You, Lord. You are my God in whom I trust. You are my King, my Lord, my Savior, my Healer and my Friend. I worship You, Lord. I praise You and thank You for being my Lord. Thank You for being my Healer. Thank You for being my Savior. Thank You for loving me. You are the best of the best. You are the greatest of the great. You are an awesome God. You are the only true God. You are mine and I am Yours. I can't live without You. You are my everything. You are my all in all. I'm desperate for You, Lord. Stay close, Lord, stay close.

"I am here, child. I am always close to you. I will never leave you nor forsake you."

I don't know what I would do, Lord, if I didn't know that. I guess I'd walk in all kinds of fear. Thank You for the knowledge that You are always with me. I know that it's true.

"I love you, precious one. I love for you to come into My presence. You are special to Me. You are My precious gem."

Lord, I delight myself in You.

"I know you do, and that blesses Me so much. I see your heart, and I know your love for Me. It is pure and genuine."

Lord, I want to please You. I want everything in my life to be pleasing to You. Make me like You, Jesus. Let there be none of me and all of You. I pray that people would see You in me.

'They do, child. They do. Continue to walk in love, and they will always see Me in you."

Fill me with Your love and compassion, Lord. Fill me with forgiveness, mercy, and faithfulness. I want to be like You. I want to love like You love. Pour out Your love on me, and let it flow through me to others. Let my heart be filled with Your love, so that love is all that comes out of me. Holy Spirit, come and be my guide today. Order my steps and help me as I do my job. Give me wisdom, knowledge, understanding, and discernment as I am working. Help me to bless others with what You bless me with, from this job. Help Jimmy and me both to be a blessing wherever we go. Lord, I pray also for You to show me things I can give out of this house. I want to give to the garage sale because the proceeds are going

October 17, 2011

to Israel. Lord, I pray for Israel right now. Forgive me for not praying more often for Israel. I pray for peace and for the people of Israel to know You personally. I pray for a move of Your Holy Spirit across Israel and the whole world wherever there are Jews. I pray for them all to come to a saving knowledge of You, Jesus. I pray for America, too, Lord. Forgive us of our sins, and heal our land. Bring America back to You. I pray for a move of Your Holy Spirit across this land that will bring America back to You. Lord, show me my part. Show me what You want from me. Make me a person that leads people to You. Make my life a trophy for You. Help Jimmy and me to come to a place where our lives are speaking to others about You and Your power. Turn our tests and trials into testimonies so that we may shine for You. Take us to the other side of the trials we have been going through in faith. Take us to the other side with victory. Let us be a light for You, Lord. Let our lives speak for You. Show us our part. Draw us nearer to You. Give Jimmy and me each a new hunger for Your Word. Give our children and grandchildren a new hunger for You and Your Word. Draw our family closer to You. I pray that our family will always be a light for You. I pray that Your will be done on earth as it is in Heaven, in our family. Open up Heaven and rain down on our family; rain on our home and on our children's homes. Rain down Your Holy Spirit and Your blessing.

Lord, I pray for Jimmy today. I ask You to be with him today as he walks through this day. I pray for strength and healing in his body. I pray for You to fill him with Your joy. Let the joy of the Lord be his strength. Draw him closer to You, Lord. I pray for him to feel that love for You that he felt back in 2005 when he had that experience with You. Rain on him, Lord. Pour out Your Spirit on him. I pray that You give him a new passion to write. I thank You that he is a writer and the author of many books. Bless him, Lord. Bless him to be a blessing. I pray for creative miracles in his body; in his feet, his knees, and his shoulders. Give him new knees and new feet so that he can run and not grow weary, so that he can walk and not faint. I thank You that You bore his pain on the cross. Take away his pain. I know that it is done. I thank You for taking his pain on that cross. I pray for the manifestation of what has already been done. I thank You for the creative miracles. I thank You for the healing. I stand in faith for him. Lord. Bless him and use him for Your purposes. Use us both for Your purposes. We are Yours. Have Your way in us. Your will, not ours, be done in what we do and where we go to serve You. I love You, Lord.

Speak to me this morning through the eyes of my heart. I will watch to see what You have to say to me this morning.

"You are precious, oh so precious, My child. If

you only knew how much it blesses Me that You came to spend this time with Me. I love when you come and sing to Me. I love when you dance for Me. I love you, little one. I love when you tell Me how much you love Me and what I mean to you. Oh, how that blesses Me! You ARE pleasing to Me. Thank you for loving Me."

Lord, I don't just love You. I am desperate for You and for Your love.

"I know, child. I know that about you."

I need You, Lord. I need You every minute of every day.

"I know, and I am here with you always. You make Me smile. Your personality makes Me smile. You are funny, child. I made you that way, and you make Me laugh. You make others laugh too. You bring life to others."

That's what I want to do, Lord. I want to bring life and healing to others.

"You do. You bring more healing to others than you realize. You are a blessing to many. I am using you and have been using you for a very long time to bring healing to others. And you will continue to bring healing to others on an even greater scale. That is a gift I have given you. People light up when you are with them. Continue to love others, and share My love with them. Let My love flow through you to

others. So many people need to be loved. Like Helen, she needs to be loved. Take time when you are not being paid, and go see her. It blesses her for you to come. Don't ever be afraid to give. I will always bless and multiply your giving. So even when it seems to be your last dollar, know that it isn't. I will always provide for you. You have lots to give, and I mean that in more ways than one. Give, child. Love others. Prefer others above yourself."

Thank You, Lord. Is there anything else You want to say to me this morning?

"Go to My Word and spend some time there. I will be with you."

Yes, Lord. I will. Thank You for speaking to me this morning.

"My pleasure. I am always speaking to you. Listen for My voice."

I will. I love You.

"I loved you first."

Yes, You did. Thank You.

DAY 14

DECEMBER 22, 2011

Good morning, precious Lord Jesus.

"Good morning, My precious one. This has been a good time together this morning; hasn't it?"

It has, Lord. Thank You for waking me up and for spending time with me this morning. I love You so much. Forgive me for letting busyness keep me from coming to You every morning. Help me to be more disciplined to seek You first every day. There is nothing in my life that is more important than that, yet I put things in that place. I am so sorry for that, Lord. Forgive me.

"You are forgiven, My child. Come to Me often and let's sup together. I love it when you come into My presence. You are precious to Me. Spending time with you blesses Me."

Lord, teach me how to come into Your presence.

"You know how. Just come. There's no formula.

Just come. I am always here waiting and ready to be with you. Jim was right when he said that My love language is spending time together. I love it when My people give Me their time."

Well, here I am, Lord, Here is my time this morning. It's Yours. Have Your way in me this morning. Fill me up with Your love, compassion, and care for others. Help me to be Your hands and feet. Lord, I want to be like You. Your Word says that I am made in Your image. Therefore I am like You, right?

"That is right. You are a work in progress. You are a child of the Most High God. You are My sister and My friend. You are royalty. You are filled with My Spirit. Walk in the Spirit and not in the flesh. The flesh wars after the Spirit to have control of you. Let My Spirit control you always, and you will walk in My ways. You will look like Me. You will heal the sick, cleanse the lepers, heal the brokenhearted, raise the dead, and set the captives free. You will do these things in My name. I am going to use you in many ways in My Kingdom. You ARE My hands and feet. Let Me fill you to overflowing."

Fill me, Lord. Fill me Holy Spirit. Lord, there is a reason that I have such a desire to heal others. You put that in me. I know it because not everyone has that desire.

December 22, 2011

"Yes, My desires have become your desires; The enemy would like to distract you and give you worldly desires. But stay close to Me and to My Word, and you will fulfill the desires of My heart on this earth."

Oh, Lord, that is what I want. I want to fulfill the desires of Your heart. Healing is the desire of Your heart, isn't it?

"I desire that none would perish. My will is to do the will of the Father, drawing all men to Me. My will is health, wholeness, prosperity, and plenty for all. It doesn't make Me happy to see My people in poverty. It doesn't make Me happy to see My people sick, diseased, or suffering in any way. I came to destroy the works of the devil, therefore I give you power to destroy the works of the devil around you. Heal the sick, raise the dead, cleanse the lepers, set the captives free, and bring healing to the brokenhearted. Bless those that curse you. Pray for those that spitefully use you. Give and it shall be given to you; pressed down, shaken together, and overflowing will men give into your bosom. Walk in love wherever you go. Don't let people get you out of love. No matter what others say or do, walk in love. Let peace be your rule when you aren't sure which way to go; My peace will guide you. Be watchful of the wiles of satan—he wants to set traps for you everywhere you go. Bless and do not curse. That is My way; cursing is his way. Walk in My ways, and you will fulfill all that I have

put you on this earth to accomplish. Your latter days will definitely be greater than your former days. That is true for Jim also. He will do great things while he is on this earth. Don't let age make you think that I don't still have much for you and him to do. I have a great work for both of you. Be cleansed and purified so that you may walk in My ways. My ways are higher than your ways. Do you want to walk in them?"

You know I do, Lord. I want our lives to be a testimony of You, Jesus. I want everything that we have been through to be part of our testimony of Your greatness.

"It is, and it will be. Your lives will testify of Me greatly. Tell others of My wonders. Don't be afraid to speak of what I have done for you."

Lord, help me to truly internalize that scripture in *Revelation 19:10 For the testimony of Jesus is the spirit of prophecy.*

"I am. Testify of Me by telling others of My wonders every day. It will cause the same to come about in others' lives. Faith will arise, and I will be able to do much in the lives of the hearers. When you speak of the wonders of God, it sets the stage for more of the same. Testify, child. Testify."

Lord, at one time You told me to write down things that I knew of that You had done. I wonder if I

December 22, 2011

lost that when my computer crashed.

"It's not lost. You can recall it, just as you can recall the things on faith and love. It is in you. I am in you and I know all things. Draw from My Spirit in you. Take some time right now, and write down things that I have done in your life or in the lives of others you know."

I will, Lord. Thank You.

Day 15

January 18, 2012

    Precious Lord Jesus! I love You so much. I honor You, and I bless You. I give You all of me. You can have all of my desires. Make Your desires my desires. I want Your will and Your ways in my life. I want to be like You, Jesus. Make me like You. Help me to walk like You, talk like You, live like You, heal like You, bless like You, love like You, and have compassion like You. Put Your passion for the lost in me. Help me to live for You—totally and completely. As with Jabez, bless me indeed, so that I may bless others. Enlarge my territory so that I can touch lives in more places. Enlarge Jimmy's territory. Bless him indeed, so that he may be a blessing all the days of his life. Fill us with Your love. I want more and more of You, Jesus, in my life. Fill me with YOU, Jesus. I want people to see Your eyes when they look into mine. I want people to see, know, and feel Your love when they are with me. Pour out Your Spirit on me and on Jimmy, so that we may spread Your love to everyone we come in contact with. I bless You, Lord. I honor You, and I lift Your name on High. Bless the name of Jesus. I adore You, Father. I love You with all my heart, all my soul, all my strength, and all my mind. Holy Spirit, I love You, and I honor You. I ask You to have Your way in our meeting tonight. You are welcome in our home, and You are certainly welcome in Kerri's home. Thank You for coming and ministering to the needs of the people there. If anyone comes who needs ministry, I pray that You won't let them leave without receiving just what they need. Pour out Your Spirit on us tonight. Set us on fire for You. I pray for Your presence tonight like never before in any of our Home Church meetings. Come, Holy Spirit.

Holy Spirit, speak to me now through the eyes of my heart. What does my Father want to say to me today?

"Be still; I am here. Listen; I am here with you, child. You are not alone, nor will you ever be alone. I am with you always. I am your Strength, your Protector, and your God in whom you trust. And because you trust Me, I will deliver you from the snare of the fowler. Though you stumble, you will not fall. I give My angels charge over you to keep you in all your ways. My Word is your strength. Attend to My Word. When you are attending to My Word, you

January 18, 2012

are attending to Me. I am the Word. When you are speaking My Word, you are literally speaking Me into the situation."

Wow, what a revelation! Thank You, Lord.

"When you speak My Word, you are bringing Me on the scene. My Word became flesh. Know My Word; speak it into every situation you come upon. Speak life even when others are speaking death. Walk in My Word. Live in My Word. Don't let it depart from your mouth. Keep it within the midst of your heart. Keep it in front of you, so that your eyes may gaze upon it. My Word is I AM. When you are gazing upon My Word, you are gazing upon Me. I and My Word are one and the same. So when you go to My Word, look at is as coming to spend time with Me because that is what you are doing. Let My Word get in you. The more My Word gets into your heart, the more I get into your heart."

That puts a whole new light on reading the Bible.

"Yes, it does. I am the Bible."

Lord, as I go to Your Word, show me what You want me to share with the kids Friday.

"I will."

You know I want to make an impact on each one of them.

"I know, and you will."

I want to make an impact on the adults there also.

"You will."

Show me how to present whatever I am to share in a way that holds the interest of everyone.

"I will."

"I don't want to add drama or acting just for show, but I do want to keep their attention."

"You will."

Thank You, Lord. I trust that You will give me all that I need. Is there anything else You want to say to me before I go to Your Word?

"I'll say it there. Go."

I'm going now. Bless You, Lord.

Bless you, My child.

Day 16

February 15, 2012

Good morning, precious Lord.

"Good morning, My Child."

Father, I adore You, I honor You, and I bless You. You are my God in whom I trust. I love You with all my heart, all my mind, all my strength, and all my soul. You are everything to me. You are my Abba (Daddy) Father. Thank You, Father, for sending Jesus for me. Jesus, I love you, and I adore You. I honor You, and I bless You. You are my everything and my all in all. You are my Lord and Savior, my King and my God in whom I trust. I praise You, Jesus. I love You. Thank You for interceding for me every day to my Father. Thank You for sending Your Holy Spirit to be with me every day, everywhere I go. Holy Spirit, thank You for always being here with me. Holy Spirit, speak to me this morning through the eyes of my heart. What does my Father want to say to me this morning?

"My precious one, I will never leave you or forsake you. You do not have to be nervous. You do not have to fear anything. You are Mine, and I take care of those who are Mine. I have already gone before you and have given you favor with all those you come in contact with. You have favor, child. Walk in that favor. Let insecurity and inferiority leave you. Let it go. Let fear at any level go. Refuse to fear. Walk in faith. You don't have to walk with faith in yourself, but with faith in Me. I will be with you, and will give you everything you need; you don't have to stress. Take what you need with you, and go in peace. You are going to enjoy your job. It will not be hard for you in any way, so stop fretting about it. You are going to like your supervisor, your coworker, and the family. They are going to be very pleased with you, and they will like you also. Remember favor. Think favor all day today. Look for My favor everywhere you go. Remember, you have preferential treatment wherever you go. Expect it. It is yours. Favor is yours. You are Mine, and Mine walk in favor. You have done what you have to do to get ready. Don't forsake gathering together with believers to stay home and worry about your afternoon. Go and pray with the ladies, trusting Me to be with you on the job. You are going to do well. Pray in the Spirit today as much as you can. It will edify you, and the fear will go. Sing and praise your Father in Heaven and peace will come upon you. My peace I give to you."

February 15, 2012

Thank you, Lord. Is there anything else You want to say to me now?

"I love you, Janet. And remember that this job is only for a season."

I love You, Lord. Thank You for always being here with me.

Day 17

March 16, 2012

Precious Lord, thank You for this time of worship this morning. I love You so much. I love Your presence, and I want more of it. That is my heart's desire. Your Word says that if I delight myself in You, that You will give me the desires of my heart. Lord, I do delight myself in You. I want more and more of You. I want to see Your face. I want to visit Heaven. I want to do all that You put me here to do. I want Your presence in my life everywhere I go. I want to always know that You are right there with me, no matter where I am. Then I will know that I will have all that I desire. Most of all I desire You, Lord. I want to walk in Your presence, and to hear Your voice more. I want to always recognize when You are speaking to me. Lord I want to be closer and closer to You. I want to learn everything there is to learn about You. Teach me about my Father, teach me about my Jesus, and teach me about You, precious

Holy Spirit. I want more of God and no more of me. I want people to see Jesus in my face and in my eyes. I want people to feel His presence when I am with them. I want to bring the Kingdom of God to everyone I come in contact with. I want to go where You want me to go, and I want to say what You want me to say. I only want to do what You want me to do, nothing more and nothing less. Help me to be like Jesus, and only say or do what my Father is saying or doing. Show me the way, Holy Spirit. Show me the way to the Spirit filled life. I want to walk in the fullness of God every day of my life. I want to be a carrier of the presence of God. Make me holy in every way, so that I will be a place for You. Let my body, this temple, be filled with You, Holy Spirit. If there is anything that needs to go, show me. Take from me what is not of You. Take any pride, self-focus, greed, doubt, unbelief, and anything else that is not of You. Make me like You, Lord. You are my standard; I want no other standard. Lord, I want to hear Your voice this morning. Speak to me through the eyes of my heart. I bless You, Lord.

"I bless you, My child. You are so very precious to Me. I love you, little one. I am pleased with you. I see your heart, and it is not divided. Come out into the deep with Me, little one."

Show me how, Lord.

March 16, 2012

"Just come. Take My hand, and don't be afraid."

(I see Jesus in the water with His hand out to me. He's washing me with the water and a gentle cloth.)

"You are Mine, child; you live for Me. I am blessing you to be a blessing. I am cleansing you and purifying you. I am anointing you."

(He's pouring something on my head.)

"I am anointing you with the oil of gladness. You have a merry heart, and a merry heart is good medicine. I want you to be able to keep that merry heart, so I am sending you power from on High. You will write; Jim will write. You will bless; Jim will bless. You will lay hands on the sick, and they will recover. Are you a believer, child?"

I am, Lord; You know I am.

"Yes, you are, and My Word never comes back to Me void. My Word says that you (the believer) will lay hands on the sick, and they will recover. I am anointing your hands. Give Me your hands."

Lord, take my hands; they are for Your service.

"Child when you feel My power in your hands you will know that I want you to pray for someone. Don't miss an opportunity to bring healing to someone."

Will it be heat, Lord?

"Yes, it will feel much like heat."

Lord, I want to bring healing to people when I touch them—even for a hug.

"You will, child. You are bringing healing to Billy; you just can't see it yet. He is being healed. Continue to pray for him and to touch him. There is power in your touch. My power is in you to heal. Heal the sick, raise the dead, cleanse the lepers, give the brokenhearted their lives back, and set the captives free. Freely you have received, freely give."

Lord, that is my desire. I want to give, and I want to walk in Your love. I want to bring life to the hurting by bringing healing to those who are emotionally or physically sick.

"You will, child. You already are."

Lord, do You want me to begin working on the scriptures for Jim's book today?

"You can; I will be with you. You can go to My Word, and begin to read and find scriptures that will fit. I will help you."

Is there anything else You want to say to me right now?

"Just go to My Word. I'll meet you there, and we'll talk more."

Thank You, Lord. I love You!! What a God You are!!!

Day 18

April 9, 2012

Hello, precious Lord God. I love You so much, Lord. I bless You, and I honor You. You are my God in whom I trust. You are my King and my Lord. You are the Great I AM. You are Jesus. You are mine, and I am Yours. Oh, thank You for letting me be Yours. I don't know what people do who don't know You. I want to help others to know You. I want to bring the Kingdom to people. Show me how, Lord. I want demonstrations of Your power to bring people to a saving knowledge of You. I want signs and wonders to follow me as I go out into the world and share You. Lord, fill me so full of You that You are who people see when they see me. Cleanse me and purify Jimmy and me of all that is not of You. Take all evil from our midst. I read in Bill Johnson's book that the root word in the Hebrew for evil is pain, disease, and poverty. Lord, take those evils from us. You are our refuge and our fortress, our God in whom we trust. Surely, You shall deliver us from the snare of the fowler (which is evil, of course). Thank You for delivering Jimmy, me, and our family from evil. Thank You for rebuking the devourer for our sake and for abundant life. Thank You for our family and our godly friends. Lord, show us how to help the poor more. Give Jimmy and me ideas to minister to the poor and needy—Your ideas. Lord, I want to be part of bringing Heaven to earth. Show me the way. Draw me so close to You that I can sense Your presence always. I know You are always with me, but I have a desire to see Your manifested presence all around me. I pray for our home—that it be a place of Your presence. Lord, when Your presence is here, there is freedom, healing, and deliverance. Bring that to our home. Help us to be Your hands and feet so that we may bring freedom, healing, and deliverance to others. I pray for my husband, for deliverance from pain in his physical body. I call forth healing, right now, in Your precious Name, Jesus. Thank You for healing Jimmy from the top of his head to the soles of his feet, so that he can fulfill all that You have put him here to do. I thank You for delivering us from debt and always providing for all of our needs. You are so faithful, so kind, and so merciful. Lord, I thank You for Your mercy, but I also ask that You help us to be holy, as You are holy. Purify us, Lord. I want to be like You—loving like You and giving like You. I want to bring You to others.

April 9, 2012

Lord, speak to me this afternoon. What do You want to say to me right now?

"My kingdom is inside you; you can bring it wherever you want. You can release it wherever you want, by faith. Let My Kingdom come and My will be done on earth as it is in Heaven. You already have the keys to the Kingdom. Take the risk. Use the keys. Pray for people in need. Bless people; love people. Go in My name, and others will know that I live."

I feel like I need some kind of course or someone to teach me.

"I will teach you. Just do the Kingdom: Love, give, bless, heal the sick, raise the dead, and set the captives free. Don't be afraid to tell them that I will heal them before you pray for them. I will back you up."

Wow, that's risky!

"You have to be willing to take risks. You have to be willing to be different, and to be persecuted for My sake. When you start doing what I did, persecution will come. But don't stop, because the more you step out, the more power will come."

Show me where to begin, Lord.

"I will. Listen and watch for what I have to say to you, and then obey. Don't ever be afraid to pray for someone. I will direct your steps. It is My will for you

to bring Heaven to earth. I always back up My will. Your will, child, is to fulfill all the purposes I have put you on earth to fulfill. I love you.

Day 19

May 7, 2012

Good morning, my precious Lord Jesus.

"Good morning, My little one."

Lord, I praise You, I honor You, and I bless You.

"Yes, you do bless Me, child. You make Me smile. You are the apple of My eye. I treasure these times with you."

I treasure them too, Lord. I am sorry that I let busyness get in the way of time with You. You are so wonderful and so kind. Your presence is the best!!! I love Your presence. I love knowing You are right here with me, and that You go with me wherever I go. I don't ever want to be without You.

"I don't ever want to be without you, My child."

Lord, thank You for all that You do in our lives. Thank You for Your mercy and Your forgiveness. Help me to walk in that mercy and forgiveness. Help me not to judge, but to love. Help me to not be critical, but encouraging not only to my husband, but everyone I come in contact with. Help me to not engage in any coarse joking, but to only let words that edify and build up come out of my mouth. Help me to take my thoughts captive when they don't line up with Your Word. Help me to walk in Your Word all the days of my life, meditating on it day and night. Help me to know it and have it in my heart, so that when I need to I can speak it out. Help me to speak only life into all situations I come upon. Help me to be so full of You, Jesus, and so full of Your love that it can't help but come out of me. I want to walk in love—true, godly love. Cleanse me and purify me of all unrighteousness, so that I may walk as You walked on this earth. I want to be so full of Your Spirit that if there is a need, I can meet that need by Your power and might. Lord, have Your way in Jimmy and me. Have Your way in our marriage and in our finances. Your will be done, and Your Kingdom come, in our lives as it is in Heaven. I want Your will for us. Order our steps. Don't let either of us go to the right if You want us to go left. Don't let either of us say anything that You wouldn't want us to say. Help us, Lord, because without Your grace and power we wouldn't be able to do anything. I pray for You, Holy Spirit, to hover over Jimmy and bring him back to his Bible reading and spending time in Your presence. I know he talks to You every day. I

May 7, 2012

know he has time with You while I am still sleeping, but he has drifted away from reading the Bible again, just as I do at times. Forgive us, Lord and draw us back to a daily encounter with Your Word. Give each of us a new hunger for Your Word and for Your presence. We need You, Lord, so that we may walk in Your ways. I pray that Jimmy and I, our children, and children's children will fulfill all the purposes that You have for each of us. I pray for my sisters and brothers and their families to know You. Lord, send laborers into their lives to tell them how much You love them. If I am supposed to do it, then I pray for the opportunity to do so. I pray also for You to prepare their hearts to receive Your love for them.

Lord, I have said enough. What do You want to say to me this morning?

"You are precious to Me, child. I am going to use you in ways you haven't even imagined. You are a vessel that I can work through, and I am preparing you for a powerful work. All that you desire is coming to pass. You and Jim are going to step into a new level of ministry. Just put Jim in My hands. I am working things out in him. He's O.K. He will fulfill all that I have for him to do. Don't worry about your finances, because I have them in My hands. Just do what you know to do. Pray the Word, give, and stand—I'll take it from there. Continue with your Bible study. It will change you. Don't step back or

give up, because I have much to show you through it. Go with Carol and Gwen and have a blessed time in Me. Have fun. Enjoy your time away and don't worry about money. Let it go."

Is there anything else right now, Lord?

"Go in peace. You will have a good day with Billy. Enjoy it. Be blessed, My child. Know that I love you with a deep, deep, love. Know that you are so very precious to Me, and that I have your back. As well as having your back, know that I go before you to prepare your way."

Lord, go and be with Jimmy also today. Order his steps. Go before him, and cover his back too.

"I am, child. No need to worry; just stand in faith for all that you ask."

Thank You, Lord, and thank You for this time. I want to get into Your Word, but it may be after I walk, if Penny calls. Please don't let me neglect that time with You.

"I won't. I'll see you in My Word."

Day 20

June 1, 2012

Lord, I have this song on my heart this morning: "I worship You, Almighty God. There is none like You. I worship You, Oh, Prince of Peace. That is what I long to do. I give You praise, for You are my righteousness. I worship You, Almighty God. There is none like You."

Lord, there is truly none like You. You are my all in all. You are my everything. I love You so much. Father I love You with all my heart, all my mind, all my strength, and all my soul. Jesus, I love You with all my heart, all my soul, all my mind, and all my strength. Holy Spirit, I love You with all my heart, all my soul, all my mind, and all my strength. I praise You and honor You, Lord. I bless You, Jesus. I want to be in Your presence. I want to be closer to You. Come and sup with me; commune with me. Come, Holy Spirit, and tell me what my Lord has to say to me today.

"I love you, precious one. You are the apple of My eye. I adore you. Your love for Me blesses Me. I live for that love. That is why I created you. I so desire to have a relationship with you. I long to be with you. I think about you. You are always on My mind. I know that's hard to comprehend because the world is so big, and there are so many people I have on My mind. But trust Me, Janet, you are always on My mind. I love it when you drop everything and come sit at My feet. Don't ever stop coming. Draw near to Me, and I will draw near to you. You have desired many things, and those desires are things I have put inside you. Stand on My Word, and you will see all that you have believed come to pass. Janet, you delight yourself in Me, therefore I will give you the desires of your heart. Don't be afraid to ask for anything. I am here, child. All that I have is yours. Trust Me. Come to Me. Believe My Word, and take it as your own. Speak it out. Meditate on it, knowing that it never comes back void. My Word is stronger than a two-edged sword. Think about that, child. Think about wielding a two-edged sword at something that was in your way."

Like that dog barking at me the other day?

"That's right. Now think about what happened when you told Him to stop in the name of Jesus, and he did. That's just what I am talking about. Speak to your mountains with the Word of God, and your

mountains will have to move. Look what you could have done with a two-edged sword with that dog. Well, My Word is much more powerful than that. I am pleased that you have been in it day and night. Continue in My Word every chance you get. It will bring you life. Meditate on it. Speak it out. Believe it. It's life to you."

Thank You, Lord. I praise You, I honor You, and I bless You.

"I bless you, little one."

Day 21

July 15, 2012

Good morning, precious Lord.

"Good morning, My child."

Lord, I praise You this morning. I lift Your name on high. I love You, Lord Jesus. You are my King and my Lord. Thank You for dying for me. Thank You for loving me so much that You were obedient even to the cross. You are so wonderful, so kind, so compassionate and so loving. You are so forgiving and so merciful. You are the Great God in all the earth. You are my Father and my Friend. Thank You, Holy Spirit, for waking me up this morning. Thank You for this time with my precious Lord. Holy Spirit, teach me how to worship Jesus in Spirit and in Truth. I want to be a worshiper. I want to be a lover like You, Jesus. Fill me up with Your Spirit. Fill me with Your love, Your compassion, Your mercy, and Your power. Make me like You, Jesus. Cleanse me and purify me of all unrighteousness. Take my life, and use it for Your purposes. I am Yours. My life is Yours, Jesus. My body is Yours. Use me, Lord. Use me in Your Kingdom to bring souls to You and to bring healing and deliverance. My hands are Yours. My feet are Yours. Lead me and guide me; let my steps always be ordered by You, Lord. Let my mouth only speak Your words and not my own. I die to myself, Lord. I no longer live, but You live in me. I crucify my flesh and live in You, Lord. Take my life, and make something of it for Your Kingdom. I love You, Lord.

Speak to me this morning, Lord. I will be still and listen for Your voice. Speak to me through the eyes of my heart.

"You are precious, child. I'm using you, child, more than you know. It so pleases Me that you and Carol are out visiting My people. It pleases Me that you are ministering with Gwen at the House of Hope. It pleases Me that the three of you are praying for others. You are in My will, child. You are already working for the Kingdom, but I am taking you to an even higher place to work for Me and My Kingdom. You have been faithful in the small things. I am going to give you greater things. I love your worship of Me. Please don't stop. It so blesses Me when you take the time to worship and praise Me."

What a wonderful thing to know that I could bless You, Lord. Thank You for saying that.

July 15, 2012

"It is true, My child. Your worship truly blesses Me. Thank you for singing that song to Me. Child, continue to declare and decree things over Jim and your lives. Don't stop now. You are so close to your breakthroughs. Worship, praise, fast, pray, pray in the Spirit and stand on all that My Word says is yours. Wealth and riches are in your house. Healing and deliverance are in your house. Peace, joy, and righteousness are in your house. Your house is an embassy for Me. Many will come and be healed, delivered, and set free right in your house. Yes, I am giving you the desires of your heart to fix your house up so that it will be a beautiful embassy for Me and for My work. Continue to pray over it, and speak over it the things that My Word says. I bless the ground that you live on and all that you own."

Lord, set us both on fire for You. I want to eat, sleep and drink of You, Lord. Set a fire under my feet and under Jim's feet to live our lives totally and completely for You. I don't care how different we look to others—even to other Christians. I just want to sell out for You and You only.

Lord, about that wind?

"It's coming. Continue to call it forth. Continue to praise and rejoice for Jim's healing and all that you have believed for. Your suddenly is moments away. I can see in the spirit what you can't see, and there is a lot going on, both on your behalf and Jim's

behalf. Stand, child, on what you already know. Stand on My Word. My Word is the truth—the only truth. Everything else is but a vapor. My Word will stand firm forever. If you want to know what's true, stand on My Word."

Lord, I lift Jimmy up to You today. He has a big job to do tomorrow, and I thank You for that job. I know that the work he is doing is only temporary. I ask You to give him the strength he needs to do the job. I pray for supernatural strength and energy for him. I pray that You will protect him in the heat. Send a cool wind to keep them both protected in the heat. Cloudiness would be great too. I pray for no rain on their job, but cloudiness and a cool breeze. Bless my husband and Paul as they do this job. I pray for You to keep Jimmy safe as he does outside work of any kind. I thank You for healing him from the top of his head to the soles of his feet. I thank You that he will fulfill all the plans and purposes that You have for his life here on this earth.

Lord, before I go and make some decrees, is there anything else You want to say to me?

"Speak life. Call forth that which you desire, and believe that you have already received it. All that I have is yours. You have a great inheritance; take it child. Don't be afraid to take it. You delight yourself in Me, and I want to give you the desires of your heart. I bless you, child. Go and take your stand."

July 15, 2012

I will, Lord. Fill me up with Your Spirit as I go, and direct my words.

"I will, child. Go."

Day 22

August 25, 2012

Good morning, my precious Father God.

"Good morning, My little one."

Lord, You are so wonderful and so great. You are an awesome God. You are my God, and I trust You. You are my dwelling place. I love You with all my heart, all my soul, all my mind, and all my strength. I bless You and honor You, Father. Thank You for all that You have done for me. You are so kind and loving. Thank You for loving me so much that You sent Jesus to die for me. Thank You, Jesus, for loving me so much that You were obedient even to the cross. Thank You for the stripes that You took for me. Thank You for my healing and for all that You did for me. Thank You for my eternal life, and for delivering me from my sins. I love You so much. Thank You for interceding for me every day to my God in Heaven. Thank You for sending Your Holy Spirit to be with me always. Thank You, Holy Spirit, for never leaving me or forsaking me. Thank You for guiding me and comforting me. Thank You for giving me the power and grace to be all that God wants me to be.

Holy Spirit, speak to me through the eyes of my heart. I will be still and watch to see what You have to say to me this morning.

"I love you, precious one. You are My delight. You make Me smile, and you make Me glad. I bless you, child. I am with you always. I am glad that you desire to live a fasted life—as a woman of moderation. I will give you the grace to walk that out. I have much in store for you; you will need to walk in moderation to accomplish all that I have for you. You will lay hands on the sick and they will recover. You will trample on lions and scorpions. You will command the devil and he will flee. You will set the captives free, raise the dead, cleanse the lepers, and heal the brokenhearted. This is My will for you. You will bring freedom to many. Yes, Billy will be healed. Stand on that and believe it. I hear the prayers of his mother, and I will bring healing to him. The floodgates of Heaven have opened up to you and Jimmy. Your obedience in giving has opened a floodgate for you. Continue to stick to that commitment. I will show you each time where you are to give. Listen and be willing to do what I tell you."

August 25, 2012

I will, Lord. I'm excited about giving that money. I have no fear about not having enough. I actually have more faith that You will provide for all our needs. I love You, Lord. I want to honor You in all that I do.

"When you are obedient, faith arises. That is why it is so important to walk in obedience. Disobedience causes guilt and condemnation, and then faith wanes. Without faith it is impossible to please Me. I desire for My people to believe I am who I say I am, and that I will do what I say I will do. That is faith in a nutshell."

Lord, I believe You are who You say you are, and I believe You will do what You say You will do. Help me with any unbelief that rises up to cause me to doubt that.

"I will. I am pleased with your faith and with Jim's faith. You are going to see some great things happening very soon in your lives. I believe you are both ready. The devil is fighting you tooth and nail, but you win, not him."

Lord, I ask Your forgiveness for both Jimmy and me for putting things in our bodies—Your temples—that don't belong there. Lord, forgive us, and deliver us from our own destructions. I pray for healing in his body. Deliver him Father, also from the physical pain he has walked in for so long.

"I am, child. You and Jimmy are going to testify of My goodness and power all over the world."

All over the world??? It's hard to see past Valdosta right now, but I believe You.

"Yes, it may be hard for you to go further than your immediate area right now, but I shall intervene. You will be able to go to the ends of the earth for Me, bringing life to many. Continue to stand on all that I have spoken to you. All that you have believed is coming to pass quickly. Don't give up and don't listen to satan's lies. Just walk in truth. Worship Me in spirit and truth, and stand. Pray in the Spirit often, praise, spend time in My Word, and believe big. My power is in you, so use that power as I lead you."

I will, Lord. Lead me and guide me into wherever You want me to minister. Let me be Your hands and feet to a hurt and dying world.

"I am."

Lord, is there anything else You want to say to me right now?

"You are healed, child. Your eyes are healed, your neck is healed, and your blood pressure is healed. Walk in that healing."

Day 23

September 15, 2012

Good morning, precious Lord. I love You so much. You are so wonderful! Thank You for all You are doing in our lives, and for all You are teaching us. Thank You for teaching Jimmy and me how to live for You in lack, so that we can live for you in plenty. Thank You for all that You are doing in Jimmy right now. Thank You for Jesus, Father, and thank You for Your precious Holy Spirit. God, I don't know what I would do without You. I am so thankful that I will never have to live without You. You are the best of the best. I pray for anyone in my family who may not know You. Let them see You in Jimmy and in me. I love them and want them to know Your love for them. If we are to share the Gospel with any of them, I pray that You prepare their hearts and open the door for us. Lord, is there anything that You want to say to me right now? Speak to me through the eyes of my heart, Lord.

"I love you, precious one. I am doing a new thing in you and in Jimmy. There is no one who can be around you and not see Me in you. Walk in love. Don't let pride in at any time. Love, bless, and do not curse. Speak life, speak love, and serve. Serve your family. I will give you words when you need them. Remember My Holy Spirit is in you, and you have all that you need to share the Gospel. They need to know My love. That is what they don't know. My love is in you, so let them know you. Be My hands and feet. I am in you, and the life you live, you now live in Me. Cast your cares on Me, and walk in love wherever you go. Serve others. Bless others; prefer them above yourself. I am with you, child. And if you desire for them to know Me, know that I long for that relationship with them more than you can even imagine. Continue to pray for them, and let your light shine before them. Go, and walk in love."

Day 24

November 2, 2012

Good morning, precious Lord.

"Good morning, My child. I love you. You are the apple of My eye. Thank you for giving Me your time this morning. I will multiply it back to you. I love when you get up and spend time with Me."

I love to be with You, Lord. Thank You for always being here for me. You are so faithful and kind, and so loving and compassionate. You are so merciful and forgiving, and so wonderful and powerful. Thank You for being my Provider, my Redeemer, my Rock, my Healer and my Friend. Thank You for loving me so much. Thank You for giving strength to my body and to Jim's body. Thank You for healing us both from the top of our heads to the soles of our feet. Thank You for bringing Heaven to our home. Lord, I love You so much. I want You first in everything. I want You, Jesus, to be Lord of every area of my life. Take charge. Have Your way in me and in my life. Order my steps, and order Jim's steps. Have Your way in us. Cleanse and purify us of all that is not of You. Fill us both to overflowing with Your precious Holy Spirit. Lord, I want to walk in the fullness of Your Spirit every day. I want to know Your presence always. Is that too much to ask?

"No, it is not. You can know My presence every moment of your life."

Thank You, Lord. That is my desire. Help me to do my part, and not to let the busyness of the day get in the way of my time with You. Even in my busyness, I want to talk to You and listen to You. Give me ears to hear what You have to say to me. Help me to recognize Your voice quickly, and to obey quickly without questioning if it is You. Help me to be so sure of Your presence that I always know when You are speaking to me. Teach me Your ways, Lord. Teach me to be like You. Pour out Your love in me so that I can pass it on to others.

"I am child, I am. My love and compassion are already in you; just give it away. You have compassion for others. I will give you more as I desire you to give it away. Love others wherever you go. Prefer others above yourself, even at home with Jimmy and other family members. Always prefer them above yourself. You are blessed to be a blessing; don't ever forget your Source. Continue to give, and

it shall be given to you pressed down, shaken together and overflowing. Give of your time. Give of your clothing and sustenance. Give of your income." Love others by giving whatever it is that will meet a need."

Day 25

February 20, 2013

Precious Lord, "You are great. You do miracles so great. There is no one else like You." That song is playing, and it is so very true to what I want to say to You right now. You are so wonderful, Lord. You are so kind, so loving, so merciful, and so compassionate. You are my first love. You are my Lord and my King. You are my God in whom I trust. Lord, forgive me for not trusting You. Forgive me for running to everything but You, and for striving instead of just being at peace and waiting on You. Lord, I am so sorry for trusting in myself and in others instead of You. I am so sorry for fearing what man thinks. Lord, I want to just trust You. I have been all over the internet again looking for work, striving. I am sorry, Lord. I don't want to strive; I want to wait on You. You know that I am willing to work, but I want to do the work that You have for me to do. Lord I want to just press into You more, and wait on You. I was thinking tonight that if I was truly believing that all I have prayed for is coming to pass, I would be preparing my home, my body, and my life. I would be pressing into You more, rejoicing, not all over the internet looking for work. I want to look at our situation from the supernatural realm, not from the natural realm, because I know that it's the superior realm. I know that Your Word is superior to anything I can see in the natural. Lord, teach me to see things from the supernatural more than the natural. Teach me how to set my eyes on things above and not on earthly things. Lord, in the natural things can look grim. But Your Word doesn't make things look grim at all. If I can only believe Your Word, and I do, then things don't look grim at all. Lord, I believe. Help me with my unbelief. I know You love me so much; help me to trust in that love more. I know that You're Jehovah Jireh, my provider. Help me trust You more for my provision. Forgive me for looking to man and not to You. You are my Source, and I know that You will provide for all our needs. I don't care how You do it, Lord; I just know that You are going to do it. I know that You are going to provide for our every need and even our every desire. Empty us of ourselves. Help us to just seek first You and Your Kingdom, trusting You with the rest. Help Jimmy and me both to do that. Lord, I know that You are a merciful and forgiving God. I know that You are our Healer and Provider; therefore, I will not listen to the

February 20, 2013

lies of satan. Lord, I will trust You to change us and our circumstances—only You, Lord. You are the miracle maker. Thank You for the miracles coming our way. Teach me how to be still and know that You are God. Teach me how to "sleep in the storm" like Bill Johnson talks about. Teach me how to rest in You.

Lord, speak to me through the eyes of my heart. What do You want to say to me right now?

"Child, be still. Be at peace, resting in the knowledge of My love for you. Remember My power. In a moment, I can turn your world completely around. In a moment, I can heal Jim. Yes, I am the miracle maker, and I have miracles for you and Jim. You are going to see your miracles, but I need for you to rest. I need you to stop striving, and trust in Me one hundred percent. Give Me all that concerns you. Let Me take your cares; I need you to trust Me with your cares."

Lord, You say one hundred percent. What if I only had a mustard seed of faith? What if I could only trust You as much as a mustard seed? What then?

"You have faith, child, much more than a mustard seed. You have a lot of faith. I need you to act on it by resting in Me. Faith without works is dead. The works I need from you right now is rest. Trust in what I have said in My Word and what I

have said to you personally. I need you to exercise your faith. Stop trying to make anything happen, including a job. If I want you to work, I will give you a job. You won't have to strive to get it. Child, what if everything I have said to you is true? What if I heal Jimmy? What if I bring you money from the north, south, east and west? What if I make you wealthy? What if I anoint Jim to write many books? What if I anoint you to heal the sick, raise the dead, cleanse the lepers, set the captives free, and heal the brokenhearted? What if the things we have talked about so often come to pass? What then? What if...?"

I would not be looking for a job. I would have plenty to do.

"What if you need to prepare for these things? Yet, you are busy looking all over the internet for a job, not having time to prepare or to spend time in My presence before all these things come about."

Maybe I would miss my miracles, or not be prepared for what You have for me. Maybe You would have to give me more time to be prepared, and my miracles would be on hold. Maybe satan could get a foothold.

"I think you are getting the picture. Don't be double-minded, child. Believe and receive. Put action behind your faith. Don't journal one thing and prepare for another. Believe, just like you told

February 20, 2013

Sharon today, that you hear My voice. Truly believe that, child, because you do. What's happening is that you are being double-minded. Fear is getting a foothold. You must shut the door on fear, and believe what I have said in My Word. Believe also what I say to you when you journal or when I just speak to your heart. Believe what you declare about Jim's and your future. Don't believe what satan says."

Lord, forgive me for being double-minded. I am sorry. I don't want to be double-minded anymore. Change me, Lord. Change my heart. Show me how to act on my faith. Show me how to be still, and at the same time take authority when I am to take authority.

"I will. Continue to take captive the thoughts that satan sends your way. You have been recognizing that they are from him and that you are to take them captive. You have already been taking authority over the things he brings to your mind. That is good. That is exactly what you need to do. He is working hard to distract you and Jim from accomplishing all I have for you. But stay the course. I am not a man that I should lie. I have spoken the truth to you. Live by it. Rest in it. If you have to go back to your journaling to get built back up in your faith, do it. Read the things I have said to you. Also, spend time in My Word to build your faith, but don't do any of it by striving. Rest in the storm. Rest in Me, in all the storms that come your way. Then you will have the power to take

authority and calm the storm. Rest in My love for you."

Give me the grace to do that, Lord, Give me the enabling power to rest in You and to trust You completely. Right now, I make the decision to trust You. I pray for the power to carry that out. I give You all my concerns and all my stress. I give You my life. Have Your way in my life. It's back to the basics, isn't it? Back to letting go and letting You have the reins.

"That's exactly right. Let go of the reins."

I'm remembering the word that was spoken over me by Kelly's husband, Travis. He said that he saw me holding on to a rope and being dragged along. He said that I was to let go. Wow! I get it. I need to give you the reins. Direct my life, Lord; I give you the reins. I am letting go and letting My Heavenly Father take the reins of my life. Help me, Lord, not to take them back.

"I will. You can do it. You can let go and trust Me. I have this. I have it all. I have your finances. I have your husband's health. I have your life. I have all your concerns. I have it. I have the reins. Thank you for giving them up."

Lord, is it time to go back to bed? Is there anything else You want to say to me?

"Goodnight."

February 20, 2013

Goodnight, Daddy.

"Goodnight, daughter."

I love You.

"I loved you first."

Yes, You did. Thank You!!!

"Thank you for letting Me love you. Go now and rest in My love. Go now and sleep; I will restore your rest. You will wake up rested and rejuvenated."

Yes, Lord. Amen.

Day 26

June 2, 2013

Precious Lord Jesus, I love You, and I desire more intimacy with You. Come closer, Lord. Let me sup with You. Come and commune with me. You are the King of kings and the Lord of lords. You are my Lord and my Jesus. Lord, forgive me for all the times that I have let busyness come between You and me, and for putting anything before You. You are number one in my life. Fill me up with Your precious Holy Spirit. Come, Holy Spirit, I need You. Fill my husband up with Your Holy Spirit. Fill us so full of Jesus, that everywhere we go people will want to know who we know. Give us the words to tell others about You and about Your love for them. Take all fear of man from Jimmy and me so that we can be bold in You. Give us a new boldness to proclaim the Gospel. Lord, I so desire to bring healing and wholeness to people: physically, emotionally and spiritually. I so desire to meet the needs of others by being Your hands and feet. I know that You will give me the words to say because You've already said that in Your Word. Thank You for the words to say to bring others to a saving knowledge of You. Lord, fill me with Your love for others. Fill Jimmy and me so full of Your love that it just flows out of us—not only to each other, but to all we come in contact with. I want to be like You, Jesus. Make me more and more like You. Take away any selfishness and self-centeredness from me and from Jimmy. Make us first Christ-centered, then other-centered. Help us to prefer others above ourselves. Teach us the truth, Lord, and give us the discernment to know who the false teachers are. I pray for a Spirit of wisdom and revelation for both Jimmy and me. Lord, I pray for Jimmy's anointing to write to come on him with every step he takes and even whenever he sits in his recliner. Lord, pour out Your anointing on him. Give him the power to overcome all that satan has tried to put on Him. Deliver him from the pain in his body once and for all. I thank You, Father, that You hear my prayers. I thank You that You answer me when I call on You. I love You with all my heart, all my soul, all my mind, and all my strength. You are my God in whom I trust. Surely, You shall deliver me from the snare of the fowler and from the perilous pestilence. I praise You, Lord, and I so desire to hear from You this morning. Speak to me through the eyes of my heart.

June 2, 2013

"Be still, My precious one. Be still and know that I am God. I am always with you, child. I will never leave you or forsake you. Tell others of My love for them. Take My love and give it to others. My love is in you; pass it on. Look for ways to bless others. Look for people in need, and then meet their need. You ARE My hands and feet. Go and do good to those who I put in your path. Fear not, for I am with you. I will give you the words to say. Keep your eyes and ears open, and you will bring life to many. Everywhere you go, look for opportunities to bring life to people. Look for opportunities to bring My love to others. I bless you, child, and I anoint you. You have all that you need to bring life and healing to others. Go out into the world and do just that. I am with you. I will go before you and prepare the way. I will prepare the hearts of the people to receive what you have to say to them. You can do the treasure hunt whenever you are ready. My Word is at your disposal. Speak life to people, prophesying to them about all that I have for them. You will bring healing to many, and you will bring many to Me. My heart longs for My creation to come to Me. I need you child. I need your help. Will you help Me?"

Oh, yes, Lord, that is my desire. I will. Give me ears to hear Your voice and eyes to see all that You want me to see in the natural as well as in the spiritual. I pray for words of knowledge for people wherever I go, whether I am doing a treasure hunt or just out eating lunch. Lord, Carol, Gwen, and I want to do a treasure hunt. I pray that You give us clues as we pray and ask, ordering our steps on Wednesday to find our first treasure for You. Show us the way, Lord.

Thank You, Jesus. Is there anything else You want to say to me right now?

"Don't give up on Jim. He is going to do great and mighty things for Me. He will write the books. He is healed from the inside out, just as you have asked. He is a light for Me. I heard your prayers this morning as you sat in his chair, and I am answering each and every one. My anointing on him will be great. I am delivering him from all pain and sickness in his body."

Lord, is there a specific way I need to pray for him concerning his health?

"Speak life over him. Speak freedom from pain and sickness over him. Bind up all spirits of pain and infirmity. Call forth healing in his body. Speak My Word over him. Encourage him, don't discourage him. Have compassion on him, because it is through compassion that you will bring healing to him."

Lord, I need You to put Your compassion in me for Jimmy, as well as others. I want to love and have Your compassion so that I can bring healing to others.

June 2, 2013

"You have it. It's in you, but I am giving you an extra measure of love and compassion to help you bring life to others. Always be moved by love and compassion, not by fear. Love and compassion are from Me. Fear is from the enemy."

Lord, I pray for our nation. I repent of my sins, as well as the sins of our nation. Heal our land, and make us a God fearing nation again. I pray for a move of Your Holy Spirit across this nation. I pray also for Israel and for all Jews to come to a saving knowledge of You. Help them to know that You are their Messiah. Lord, give Jimmy and me opportunities to pray and minister to Jewish people in our community.

Lord, guide our steps today and every day. I lift up this job interview to You today. This looks like something I would enjoy doing. But Your will, not mine be done. If You want me to work for them, I pray for favor as I am speaking with the lady today. I trust that You will give me the words to say. I thank You that You are ordering our steps, and providing for our needs according to Your riches in glory. I love You, and I thank You for having Your way in our lives. Thy will be done, Thy Kingdom come, in our lives, on earth as it is in Heaven. I thank You for Heaven invading our earth. Bless You, Lord. Have a wonderful day!

Day 27

July 30, 2013

Good morning, Lord.

"Good morning, precious one."

Lord, I worship and honor You. I bless You, and I praise You. I trust You, Lord. You are the best of the best. You are my King and my Lord. You are my everything. Thank You for what You did on the cross for us and for what You did when You rose from the dead. Thank You for the power that You have given to us to make a difference in this world. Thank You for loving us so much. Thank You for the authority that You have entrusted to us to be Your hands and feet. Lord, I so desire to be Your hands and feet. I so desire to do Your will everywhere I go. Forgive me for getting frustrated and aggravated with Jimmy. Lord, I thank You for delivering him from all that satan is throwing at him. I thank You for delivering him from pain. Lord, I pray that You will not give up on him. Help him to do all that You put him here to do. I thank You for all the books that he will write. I thank You that his books will be best sellers, and that lives will be changed because of his books.

Lord, speak to me through the eyes of my heart. What do You want to say to me this morning?

"I love you precious one. I am with you always. You are never alone. You don't have to fear. Come against it whenever it raises its ugly head. Trust in Me, child. I am bigger than your fears. I am your all in all. Look to Me, not circumstances. Spend time in worship and praying in the Spirit. Spend time in My Word every day, not just here and there. Stand on My Word. Stand on My promises; they are yours, child. Stand in the gap for your husband until you see results. Believe and you will receive all that you are asking. My Word is true. It will not come back void. It is final. Don't listen to the lies of the enemy; listen only to My words. You have what you say. Don't speak what you see; speak what you desire. Spend some time in worship and prayer before your sister calls. I am with you, Janet. Fear not."

Thank You, Lord, I will go and worship now. I bless You, Lord. Is there anything else You want to say to me right now?

"Go in peace. Cast your cares on Me."

I will, Lord, Thank You.

Day 28

August 31, 2013

Good morning, my precious Lord Jesus.

"Good morning, child."

Lord, it is 5:13 a.m. I have been awake for a while. I woke up and heard You speaking to me. This is what I heard:

"Pick out 28 days of your best journaling. Put it together, and send it to Mark Virkler."

I don't have any idea why You would say 28 days, but that is what I heard. Lord, I have been looking through my journaling, and I have picked out some of it. I am not sure if I am to keep everything or just Your words. At first I thought it was just Your words I am to keep, but then I thought otherwise. I pray that You would make it clear to me which way You want it and also which days to pick. I am very sleepy and am planning to go back to bed soon. Is there anything else You want to say to me before I go lie down?

"Go and rest, and I will give you more instruction as you rest. Don't struggle with this. Just do it. It doesn't have to be perfect. Just pick 28 days."

Thank You, Lord. I am going to lie down. Speak to me, even in my sleep. I love to hear Your voice. Amen.

To the Reader

I have heard it said that one word from God can change the direction of your life. This word on August 31, 2013 was that for me. I never considered sharing, with others, my intimate time with the Lord. But when I was obedient to this word from God, I was put in a position to begin the publishing of this book. I pray that it has helped you to know just how intimate the Lord wants to be with you, because **EVERYTHING THAT MATTERS TO YOU, MATTERS TO HIM.**

Appendix A

The House of Hope

Since 2002, I have been involved with an Inner Healing Prayer Ministry. I have had the awesome privilege of walking alongside the Lord as He has brought healing, from life's deepest hurts, to many people. Early in 2010, I was asked to facilitate the Inner Healing Prayer Ministry at the South Georgia House of Hope. The House of Hope is a long term Christian recovery program for ladies overcoming drug and alcohol addiction and abuse. Most of the ladies are there between twelve to 18 months. One of the first things I noticed when ministering to these ladies was how easily they went through the ministry process and how quickly they received their healing. I attribute it to the fact that these ladies already believed that God would speak to them. They had been taught to hear God's voice from the day they began the program. The founder, Sharon Wagner, said that when she first started the House of Hope, the Lord told her that one of the most important things He wanted her to teach the ladies was how to hear His voice. After hearing that word from God she chose to make Mark and Patty Virkler's *4 Keys to Hearing God's Voice Seminar* a part of the curriculum. The ladies journal every morning and every evening. Very early in the program, the ladies at the House of Hope are clearly hearing the voice of God. Sharon believes that one word from God can do more than years of counseling.

I asked some of the ladies if they would be willing to share from their journaling for this book, and they were graciously willing. Enjoy getting to know them as you read some excerpts from their two-way journaling with our precious Heavenly Father:

Suzanne (3 months into the program)

Thank You, Father, for one more night. Father, I miss my family and friends so badly. I know that, in Your time, You will reunite me with them. I catch myself thinking about my "friends." I know that some of them I may never talk to again, and if that's Your will, I accept that. Thank You for all that You are teaching me and for placing the people here to work with me, so that I can be the woman You intended for me to be. I love You.

"Suzanne, My daughter, I will reunite your family. Everything the enemy has taken away, I will give back to you. The friends you talk about will be replaced with sisters and brothers in Christ. I am proud of you. You are working so hard on becoming a true, honest and godly daughter of the King. Keep it up, My most precious daughter. I love you. This journey will take many turns along the way, but keep your eyes on Me. Do not get distracted with what is

going on around you. Stay surrendered to Me, and let Me lead the way. You will get there! May your Father have this dance? If so, let Me lead you, and I will be your partner for eternity."

Upon completion of the program, Suzanne desires to get involved with inner healing ministry. She hopes to show other women how to overcome depression through the love of Jesus Christ.

Nicole (6 months into the program)

Father, thank You for waking me up safe and sober this morning. Thank You for another opportunity to come to know You in a deeper, more intimate way. It seems every other day I check off "forgetting God/self-reliance" on my Daily Moral Inventory. Out of all the liabilities listed, it is the one I struggle with the most. Some days it seems I can go the whole day without thinking about You. I don't want the hours between my morning devotions and evening journaling to be about me. I don't want to spend my days running off my own strength.

"Nicole, even though you've given Me control over your whole life, You are taking back bits and pieces by doing this. Both your independent spirit and your will were very strong. It took Me many years and you much heartache for it to be broken. Don't turn back now. Allow Me to be Lord in your life, not only over the big things, but the small; even the

teensy tiny. You've always wanted a man to take care of you. Why not let Me do it? I am more than capable. The opposite of this quality, "acknowledging God" is not what you think. It doesn't mean you stay in constant communion with Me. Don't be fooled; very few people are able to achieve that level of spiritual discipline without solitude. There will be a day when our fellowshipping will never cease, but it won't be today or any time soon, for that matter. Acknowledging Me means being Spirit-led. You asked Me the other day what I want you to work on, and this is it. Be sensitive to My Holy Spirit because, My precious daughter, He lives inside of you! It is He you can stay in constant communion with. If you haven't figured it out already, this isn't something you can do with your head. Acknowledging Me doesn't mean you are constantly thinking about Me. It means you are allowing My Holy Spirit to guide you, teach you, convict you, comfort you, speak for you and empower you. This is what will take your walk with Me to the next level. Doing My will simply isn't enough. I want you to let My will be done THROUGH you. I love you, and I am so proud of you. I am so proud of the progress you are making."

Nicole has just finished one year at the House of Hope and is coming upon completion. She plans to go to paramedic school, and do medical missions. She wants to bring healing, not only

physically, but spiritually, by leading others to a saving knowledge of Jesus Christ.

Katherine (3 months in the program)

Thank You for the worship last night and the work You did in me. Thank You for the rest I received last night and for waking me safely. Today is going to be rough for me since it's Gage's birthday, and I want so badly to be with him. So, Father, I feel the only way to get through this is total surrender. I am not strong enough to do this on my own. Help me, please!

"Katherine, don't try to speed through today, or you will miss what I have for you. Instead allow Me to set the pace. In your weakness today, you will find strength you never knew was in you. It's My strength. Believe that it will not falter. I know the hurt you are feeling, Katherine. But believe Me when I say Gage knows you are doing what is best. He is a very smart boy, and he knows that, after this year, you will be the mom he wants and deserves—and so do I. Today will not be hard on you. You are strong because I am strong within you. The day you see what I do will be a day of rejoicing. You are so beautiful to Me. I love you so much and remember it is okay to cry. Just don't dwell there. Love you, Papa"

Upon completion of the program, Katherine's desire is to do family missions in Brazil. She wants to show love to those who are less

fortunate than her, and to give back some of which has been freely given to her.

Jami (A few months after completing the program)

Father, I am hurting and need to hear Your voice about this situation.

"Jami, I am an effective equipper, and I am equipping you through this. I am your Mighty Protector. I am yours, and you are Mine. My love, I have loved you to death and life in Me. Now do the same for Todd. Through this I am cleansing you both from secret faults, so no more will they have dominion over either of you or your marriage. The prayers of both of you have been heard. When the two of you prayed together Saturday night, sound barriers were broken in heaven, and opening and cleaning of wounds began. All of this is not coincidence, but the path chosen and given by Me. You are a strong woman, and this, My love, you can handle and are going the right way. It will be used in the future; put your trust in Me. I am the only One who will not fail you. I will not lead you into harm, but I will lead you where I want you to go, and this path is called healing. This is the beginning of what you have longed for and prayed for. Take this chance and chain yourself to it. Through it all, I will be holding your hand. Do not think for one minute I am not with you. This time I am carrying you in My arms

allowing you to get some rest. I am pleased that you have not run. You have both been delivered from the hand of the enemy. Your choice to stay and run with Me has shot a sharp arrow in the heart of the enemy. This does not get easier from here. But, as you receive more healing, you will be able to see the entire picture more and more. Jami, I am in the midst of you, and you shall not be moved (Psalm 46:5). Be still. I will be exalted in and through this. You are My precious one in whom I delight. You have a spirit of Job, and in the end you will have it all back DOUBLE. Waters are going to burst forth in your wilderness and streams in your desert. Your parched ground shall become a pool. You are My servant. I have chosen you and have not cast you away. Do not fear; I am with you. Do not be dismayed; I am your God. I will strengthen you in this. Always, I will uphold you with My righteous hand. I am holding your right hand saying to you, 'Fear not, I will HELP you. I WILL HELP YOU.' My Glory will be your rear guard."

Jami completed the program in 2013 and is now on staff at The House of Hope. By giving back what was given to her, Jami has found that it truly is more blessed to give than receive.

<u>Haleigh</u> (A few months after completing the program)

I am sitting here on the beach watching the

sunrise. I am in awe of what You do. You're so beautiful! Thank You, Lord, for completely wrecking me yesterday and then letting me see this incredible sunrise this morning. You are so good, Daddy. Thank You so much for who You are and for showing me so much of Your goodness and love. Daddy, show me more of Your love today and for the rest of my life. Show me what no eye has seen and no ear has heard from the scripture that was shared with us this morning. I want to be completely consumed by You. What do You want to show me?

I want to show you more of my heart—the deeper places of My heart. I want to show you the strategies of Heaven, straight from My heart. You are coming closer into My heart. I am rekindling that fire inside of you. You're My beloved and I am yours. I just want to be with you. Just enjoy my presence and this journey we are on. Don't put restrictions on Me. I want to show you My plans, not the plans you've predicted in your mind. Just let me have control of everything. I have amazing things waiting, but you've got to trust Me—really trust Me. O.K.?

Daddy, I trust You. I give you my plans, my goals, and my life—future, past and present. I give up all for You. I want Your plans.

I promise that what I have for you is much better than anything you could ever come up with, Haleigh. I love you, and I want what's best for you. I am glad you allowed me to heal you yesterday. I took it away. No longer are you bound by the past. It's all wiped away. I want you to trust Me with everything. Let go and fly; don't hold onto the ledge. Just hold onto My hands of love. Don't be distracted by the ways around you. Daily, second by second you've got to focus on Me.

Haleigh completed the program in 2013 and then attended Iris Harvest School of Ministry in Mozambique, Africa. She desires to go to Cambodia as a long-term missionary to rescue young women from the sex trafficking industry.

Patty (Shortly after re-entering the program)

Dear Father, Thank You, and praise Your wonderful name! This day is what Your hands have made. I will rejoice and be glad in it.

Take all of Me in—I am in all that is around you, my child. You never have to take on the troubles of any day given. Rest in knowing I can and will take all the difficulties of your life troubles. My peace and fulfillment I give to you freely. My very presence is in all you see, taste, touch and smell. Enjoy the abundance of these simple pleasures and bask in the joy of knowing I am the maker—the author and finisher of your faith. Keep the fire kindled; just call out my name and I will be there to carry you. Fall into my arms and know that My grace is and has always been sufficient for you. My wings I place you under, and there you will find new strength. Lean into Me for your understanding. I will always make your path straight as you continue to acknowledge and trust Me. I love you my child—then, now and always.

Patty has recently returned to the House of Hope after leaving 3 months into the program. Upon completion of the program, Patty's desire is to lead a recovery group of single women, with children, whose lives have been affected by addiction.

MaryBeth (3 months into the program)

Lord, I praise and thank You for an overall good day today. Thank You for always being here when we need You. Lord, even though I know You know what's in my heart, I just want to tell You anyway. I love You, and my heart wants desperately to be close to You and to get closer and closer to You. I want to give You everything I have, Jesus—all of me. I want to seek You and find You in me. I want exactly what Psalm 139:23-24 says. Help me to attain that, Lord. Don't let me feel like I am just going through the motions because I am certain that is not in my heart. I want to give myself to You every day over and over so You can change me.

MaryBeth, My daughter, I am changing you little by little every day. The old is passing away and a new creation in My image is arising. I do know your heart, and your heart is beautiful in My eyes because you have asked me to come into it. You are not just going through the motions; that's just the enemy telling you lies. So cast that lie back down to the fiery pit where it came from. This life change you are taking, MaryBeth, is a process. It doesn't happen overnight. That would be easier, but you wouldn't get what you need to survive and not go back to your old ways. You need this time with Me because it's been a long time since you have really spent time with Me like this. And I am telling you that I like it, and I don't want it to stop. So let's just keep on spending this time together—you and Me. Then all those bad habits and bad thoughts are just going to pass away, and the things that the enemy is trying to put on you will just fall off. You, My daughter, are going to be triumphant and victorious in the name of Jesus.

Upon completion of the program, MaryBeth desires to be reunited with her three children. She hopes to instill in them the lessons she's been taught at the House of Hope, helping them to find their identity in Christ and raising them in His ways.

Appendix B

You Can Hear God's Voice

By Mark and Patti Virkler
co-authors of *4 Keys to Hearing God's Voice*
and *Dialogue with God*

Christianity is unique among religions, for it alone offers a personal relationship with the Creator beginning here and now, and lasting throughout eternity. Jesus declared, "This is eternal life—that they may *know God*" (Jn. 17:3). Unfortunately, many in the Church miss the great blessing of fellowship with our Lord because we have lost the ability to recognize His voice within us. Though we have the promise that "My sheep hear My voice," too many believers are starved for that intimate relationship that alone can satisfy the desire of their hearts.

I was one of those sheep who was deaf to his Shepherd until the Lord revealed four very simple keys (found in Habakkuk 2:1,2) that unlocked the treasure of His voice.

Key #1 – God's voice in your heart often sounds like a flow of spontaneous thoughts.

Habakkuk knew the sound of God speaking to him (Hab. 2:2). Elijah described it as a still, small voice (I Kings 19:12 NKJV). I had always listened for an inner audible voice, and God does speak that way at times. However, I have found that usually, God's voice comes as spontaneous thoughts, visions, feelings, or impressions.

For example, haven't you been driving down the road and had a thought come to you to pray for a certain person? Didn't you believe it was God telling you to pray? What did God's voice sound like? Was it an audible voice, or was it a spontaneous thought that lit upon your mind?

Experience indicates that we perceive spirit-level communication as spontaneous thoughts, impressions and visions, and Scripture confirms this in many ways. For example, one definition of *paga*, a Hebrew word for intercession, is "a chance encounter or an accidental intersecting." When God lays people on our hearts, He does it through *paga*, a chance-encounter thought "accidentally" intersecting our minds.

Therefore, when you want to hear from God, tune to chance-encounter or spontaneous thoughts.

Key #2 – Become still so you can sense God's flow of thoughts and emotions within.

Habakkuk said, "I will stand on my guard post..." (Hab. 2:1). Habakkuk knew that to hear God's quiet, inner, spontaneous thoughts, he had to first go to a quiet place and still his own thoughts and emotions. Psalm 46:10 (NKJV) encourages us to be still, and know that He is God. There is a deep inner knowing (spontaneous flow) in our spirits that each of us can experience when we quiet our flesh and our minds. If we are not still, we will sense only our own thoughts.

Loving God through a quiet worship song is one very effective way to become still. (Note II Kings 3:15.) After I worship and become silent within, I open myself for that spontaneous flow. If thoughts come of things I have forgotten to do, I write them down and dismiss them. If thoughts of guilt or unworthiness come, I repent thoroughly, receive the washing of the blood of the Lamb, putting on His robe of righteousness, seeing myself spotless before God (Is. 61:10; Col. 1:22).

To receive the pure Word of God, it is very important that my heart be properly focused as I become still because my focus is the source of the intuitive flow. If I fix my eyes upon Jesus, the intuitive flow comes from Jesus. But if I fix my gaze upon some desire of my heart, the intuitive flow comes out of that desire. To have a pure flow I must become still and carefully fix my eyes upon Jesus. Again, quietly worshiping the King, and receiving out of the stillness that follows quite easily accomplishes this.

Fix your gaze upon Jesus (Heb. 12:2), becoming

quiet in His presence and sharing with Him what is on your heart. Spontaneous thoughts will begin to flow from the throne of God to you, and you will actually be conversing with the King of Kings!

Key #3 – As you pray, fix the eyes of your heart upon Jesus, seeing in the Spirit the dreams and visions of Almighty God.

Habakkuk said, "I will keep watch to see," and God said, "Record the vision" (Hab. 2:1,2). Habakkuk was actually looking for vision as he prayed. He opened the eyes of his heart, and looked into the spirit world to see what God wanted to show him. This is an intriguing idea.

God has always spoken through dreams and visions, and He specifically said that they would come to those upon whom the Holy Spirit is poured out (Acts 2:1-4, 17).

I had never thought of opening the eyes of my heart and looking for vision. However, I have come to believe that this is exactly what God wants me to do. He gave me eyes in my heart to see in the spirit the vision and movement of Almighty God. There is an active spirit world all around us, full of angels, demons, the Holy Spirit, the omnipresent Father, and His omnipresent Son, Jesus. The only reasons for me not to see this reality are unbelief or lack of knowledge.

In order to see, we must look. Daniel saw a vision in his mind and said, "I was looking...I kept looking...I kept looking" (Dan. 7:2,9,13). As I pray, I look for Jesus, and I watch as He speaks to me, doing and saying the things that are on His heart. Many Christians will find that if they will only look, they will see, in the same way they receive spontaneous thoughts. Jesus is Emmanuel, God with us (Matt. 1:23). It is as simple as that. You can see Christ present with you because Christ *is present with you.* In fact, the vision may come so easily that you will be tempted to reject it, thinking that it is just you. But if you persist in recording these visions, your doubt will soon be overcome by faith as you recognize that the content of them could only be birthed in Almighty God.

Jesus demonstrated the ability of living out of constant contact with God, declaring that He did nothing on His own initiative, but only what He *saw the Father doing, and heard the Father saying* (Jn. 5:19,20,30). *What an incredible way to live!*

Is it possible for you to live out of divine initiative as Jesus did? Yes! Fix your eyes upon Jesus. The veil has been torn, giving access into the immediate presence of God, and He calls you to draw near (Lk. 23:45; Heb. l0: 19-22). "I pray that the eyes of your heart will be enlightened...."

Key #4 – Journaling, the writing out of your

prayers and God's answers, brings great freedom in hearing God's voice.

God told Habakkuk to record the vision (Hab. 2:2). This was not an isolated command. The Scriptures record many examples of individual's prayers and God's replies (e.g. the Psalms, many of the prophets, Revelation).

I call the process "two-way journaling," and I have found it to be a fabulous catalyst for clearly discerning God's inner, spontaneous flow, because as I journal I am able to write in faith for long periods of time, simply believing it is God. I know that what I believe I have received from God must be tested. However, testing involves doubt and doubt blocks divine communication, so I do not want to test while I am trying to receive. With journaling, I can receive in faith, knowing that when the flow has ended I can test and examine it carefully, making sure that it lines up with Scripture.

You will be amazed when you journal. Doubt may hinder you at first, but throw it off, reminding yourself that it is a biblical concept, and that God is present, speaking to His children. Relax. When we cease our labors and enter His rest, God is free to flow (Heb. 4:10). Sit back comfortably, take out your pen and paper, smile, and turn your attention toward the Lord in praise and worship, seeking His face. After you write your question to Him, become still, fixing your gaze on Jesus. You will suddenly have a very good thought. Don't doubt it; simply write it down. Later, as you read your journaling, you, too, will be blessed to discover that you are indeed dialoguing with God.

Some final notes: Knowing God through the Bible is a vital foundation to hearing His voice in your heart, so you must have a solid commitment to knowing and obeying the Scriptures. It is also very important for your growth and safety that you be related to solid, spiritual counselors. All major directional moves that come through journaling should be confirmed by your counselors before you act upon them.

For a complete teaching on this topic, order the book *4 Keys to Hearing God's Voice* (A left Brain presentation) or *Dialogue with God* (A right brain presentation) at www.CWGministries.org or call 716-681-4896.

Prayer of Salvation

You may be reading this book and you don't know Jesus as your Lord and Savior. You can know Him as Lord and have an intimate relationship with Him. Just pray the following prayer inviting Jesus into your life:

Heavenly Father, I come to you in the name of Jesus. I ask You to forgive me of my sins and to come live in my heart. Be the Lord of my life, and fill me with your Holy Spirit. The Bible says that *Everyone who call on the name of the Lord will be saved (Acts 2:21),* and *If you confess with your mouth Jesus as Lord, and believe in your heart that God has raised him from the dead, you will be saved. (Romans 10:9).* I am taking you at your Word. I confess Jesus as Lord, and I believe in my heart that You raised Him from the dead. Thank You, Jesus, for coming into my heart and being Lord of my life. Amen

My Prayer for You

Father, I pray for those that read this book—that they would come to know You as Abba Father and Friend. I pray for them to have a more intimate relationship with You, communing with you daily. I pray for You to pour out Your Spirit on them, and that they feel the depth of Your love as they hear Your voice like never before. I also pray that they would know that everything that matters to them, matters to You. In Jesus name I pray, Amen.

ABOUT THE AUTHOR

Janet grew up in Tampa, Florida, and moved to South Georgia in 1976 where she taught Special Education for 25 years. On Easter Sunday in 1982, Janet gave her life to the Lord. She loves to share stories of how God has made a difference in her life and in the lives of those around her. She is a long standing member of New Covenant Church in Valdosta, Georgia. For the past 12 years Janet has been involved in an Inner Healing Prayer Ministry at church, as well as in the community. She enjoys ministering and bringing God's healing power to others.

One of Janet's greatest joys is spending time with her family—her husband, Jimmy, their two daughters, Melody and Nancy, their sons-in-law, and their 6 grandchildren. Something they enjoy doing together is going on family camping trips.

References

Bevere, John. <u>Drawing Near—A life of Intimacy with God</u>. Nashville: Thomas Nelson, 2004

Dedmon, Kevin. <u>The Ultimate Treasure Hunt</u>. Shippensburg: Destiny Image, 2007

Hinn, Benny. <u>Good Morning, Holy Spirit</u>. Nashville: Thomas Nelson, 1990, 1997

Johnson, Bill. <u>When Heaven Invades Earth</u>. Shippensburg: Destiny Image, 2003

Seputis, Teresa. <u>How to Hear the Voice of God in a Noisy World</u>. Lake Mary: Charisma House, 2001

Virkler, Mark and Patti. <u>Dialogue With God.</u> Gainesville, Florida: Bridge-Logos. 1986, 2005

Virkler, Mark and Patti. <u>4 Keys to Hearing God's Voice</u>. Shippensburg: Destiny Image, 2010

Contact the Author:
jgilham@mchsi.com
For more information about
South Georgia House of Hope:
www.southgeorgiahouseofhope.org

Made in the USA
Columbia, SC
19 July 2023